CENTRE OF
THE WEB

BY THE EDITORS OF TIME-LIFE BOOKS

This edition published in 2004
by the Caxton Publishing Group
20 Bloomsbury Street, London WC1B 3JH
Under license from Time-Life Books BV.

Cover Design: Open Door Limited, Rutland UK

THE THIRD REICH
SERIES EDITOR: Thomas H. Flaherty
Series Administrator: Jane Edwin

Editorial Staff for Centre of the Web
Designer: Raymond Ripper
Picture Editor: Jane Jordan
Text Editors: Stephen G. Hyslop, John Newton, Henry Woodhead
Researchers: Karen Monks, Trudy Pearson (principals),
Philip Brandt George, Jane A. Martin
Assistant Designer: Lorraine D. Rivard
Copy Coordinator: Charles J. Hagner
Picture Coordinators: Jennifer A. Iker
Editorial Assistants: Jayne A. L. Dover

Special Contributors: Ronald H. Bailey, Lydia Preston Hicks,
Thomas A. Lewis, Richard Murphy, Brian C. Pohanka, David S. Thomson
(text); Martha-Lee Beckington, Maggie Debelius, Anthony Sheehan,
Marilyn Murphy Terrell (research); Michael Kalen Smith (index)

Editorial Operations
Copy Chief: Diane Ullius
Production: Celia Beattie
Library: Louise D. Forstall
Computer Composition: Gordon E. Buck (Manager), Deborah G. Tait,
Monika D. Thayer, Janet Barnes Syring, Lillian Daniels

Correspondents: Elisabeth Kraemer-Singh (Bonn), Christina Lieberman
(New York), Maria Vincenza Aloisi (Paris), Ann Natanson (Rome).
Valuable assistance was also provided by Barbara Hicks (London);
Sasha Isachenko (Moscow).

Title: Centre of the Web
ISBN: 1 84447 071 7

Contents

ONE

Germany's Malevolent Master

The organizers of Adolf Hitler's fiftieth birthday celebration had hoped for clear skies—"Führer weather," as sunny spring days had come to be known in the Third Reich. But April 20, 1939, dawned overcast, as if to remind Hitler's devotees that a few things remained beyond the control of the Reich's purported miracle worker. The morning clouds scarcely dampened the reverential fervor of the proceedings, however. All across Berlin, bells pealed at churches bedecked with swastikas, summoning the people to a triumphal observance of the power and glory of the man who had taken it upon himself to redeem Germany. As Field Marshal Hermann Göring, Hitler's chief lieutenant, put it that morning to an appreciative Führer and prominent members of the regime, this was a day for Germans to reaffirm their faith "in the word of Adolf Hitler. God sent him to us at the right moment—now we pray God he may keep him safe and bless his work."

To signal the importance of the occasion, the National Socialist government had granted the nation's workers a paid holiday, guaranteeing a massive turnout for the great parade in Berlin that would climax the carefully orchestrated festivities. For days, German newspapers had abounded with tributes to Hitler and exhortations to the populace to rejoice and give thanks. Presents had poured into the Chancellery from every corner of the Reich: Along with pistols, knives, and daggers, there was a live eagle—the symbol of German might—for Hitler to release in his beloved Bavarian mountains. Peasants sent their handiwork, housewives their baked goods. The women of Westphalia knitted 6,000 pairs of socks for the Führer's soldiers; his World War I infantry regiment assembled a photographic history of the old outfit.

Members of the Nazi inner circle competed hotly to come up with the most memorable present: a painting by Titian from Walther Funk, president of the Reichsbank; a festival of German films from Propaganda Minister Joseph Goebbels, a fellow movie lover; a prototype of the new people's car, the *Volkswagen*, from Robert Ley, leader of the Labor Front. On behalf of the party, Deputy Führer Rudolf Hess presented a rare collection of letters penned by the eighteenth-century Prussian monarch, Frederick the

An affable Adolf Hitler links hands with youngsters during his fiftieth birthday celebration on April 20, 1939. Hitler was aware that such scenes made him seem less forbidding, and an associate wrote that he tried to treat children in a "paternally friendly fashion" but "never managed to be very convincing."

Great, one of Hitler's heroes. On the eve of his birthday, the Führer was serenaded at bedtime by a choir drawn from his own palace guard, elite members of Heinrich Himmler's Schutzstaffel, or SS. He awoke the next morning to the murmur of two million Berliners jockeying for position along the five-mile-long Via Triumphalis, a majestic new boulevard transfixing the city from east to west.

At eleven o'clock, Hitler left the courtyard of the Reich Chancellery in an open Mercedes and motored down the boulevard, eliciting deafening cheers that rolled in waves over the black convertible as it glided slowly between towering pillars crowned with gilded papier-mâché eagles and swastikas. At 11:25, the Führer reached the reviewing stand, which was already crowded with high-ranking Nazis. There, in his plain, brown party uniform, he stood rigidly for the next four hours as the rebuilt German

The Brandenburg Gate *(above)* is illuminated for a military parade on the eve of Hitler's fiftieth birthday. During the festivities, Hitler *(top right)* accepted tributes from members of his inner circle, including his photographer, Heinrich Hoffmann *(shaking Hitler's hand)*, and physician, Theodor Morell *(waiting behind Hoffmann)*. Other well-wishers sent paintings and flowers in swastika-decorated vases to adorn the new Reich Chancellery *(bottom right)*.

military machine—the ultimate source of his far-reaching authority—rolled by in stately splendor.

Across the avenue, behind the fluttering regimental banners of more than 300 army units, the Polish military attaché anxiously scribbled notes from his seat amid the diplomatic gallery as 40,000 of the Wehrmacht's troops goose-stepped past, accompanied by horse cavalry and motorized units, huge tractor-drawn cannon, and more than 100 tanks. The attaché had ample cause to be concerned, for armed intimidation had recently brought Austria and Czechoslovakia under Hitler's thumb and Poland risked a similar fate. As if to emphasize the point, many of the tanks on review bore the names of places freshly incorporated into the German Reich—Prague, Karlsbad, Memel. Overhead flew omens of future exploits, squadrons from Göring's vaunted Luftwaffe—162 planes in all.

The German press hailed the spectacle as the "greatest parade on earth." As Goebbels underlined in a radio address to the public, the display of arms proclaimed Hitler's central accomplishment: the revival of German might. "The Reich stands in the shadow of the German sword," exulted the little propaganda chief in his ringing baritone. "The German people feel that they have, through the Führer, been raised once more to the position in the world to which they are entitled." No one on the face of the globe, declared Goebbels, could now be indifferent to the name Adolf Hitler.

For once in his career as Nazi Germany's impresario of distortion, Goebbels was stating a fact. It would have been difficult to exaggerate Hitler's importance on that April morning. He stood near the pinnacle of his power, the protagonist of one of the most remarkable and unlikely political success stories in history. Few men had ever risen so high from a position so obscure. Just two decades earlier, the world had been not merely indifferent to Hitler but blissfully ignorant of his existence. He had passed his thirtieth birthday unheralded, an embittered Austrian-born veteran of the recently concluded Great War who seemed destined to spend his life ranting futilely against the forces he blamed for Germany's downfall—the Jews, the communists, the democratic defeatists who had come to terms with the hated Allies. By the age of forty, he had yoked together a fanatical band of followers to spread his grim doctrine of Germanic revival through coercion at home and expansion abroad. As yet, his burgeoning National Socialist German Workers' party wielded little influence—it claimed only about 150,000 dues-paying members in April 1929—and few Germans took his pretensions to power seriously. Over the next few years, however, as the nation slid into depression and endured a series of debilitating parliamentary crises, Hitler's promise to impose order on a fragmented nation drew millions of new followers to him like filings to a magnet. By 1933, he was in a position to realize his stated goal: to abolish the "delirium of democracy and cause the people to recognize again the necessity of authority and leadership."

The absolute authority Hitler assumed over Germany that year was an extension of the unrestricted control he had exercised over the Nazi party during the decisive years of its struggle for power. In the party, Hitler's word was law, and this so-called *Führerprinzip*, or leadership principle, became the rule for Germany once Hitler was ensconced as its permanent chancellor. To be sure, not all Germans welcomed his totalitarian regime. Early on, thousands of Hitler's opponents were thrown into concentration camps, and millions more were intimidated into silence. By the mid-1930s, however, Hitler had secured the enthusiastic loyalty of the majority of Germans, thanks in large part to an economic recovery that had been fueled by his aggressive rearmament program. And as he restored German prestige and fulfilled his territorial ambitions for the Reich—beginning with the reoccupation of the Rhineland in 1936—the public attitude toward him deepened from respect to reverence. "The old trust him, the young idolize him," wrote the former prime minister of Great Britain, David Lloyd George, after visiting Germany in 1936. "It is not the admiration accorded to a popular leader. It is the worship of a national hero who has saved his country from utter despondency and degradation. He is as immune from criticism as a king in a monarchal country. He is something more: He is the George Washington of Germany—the man who won for his country independence from all her oppressors. To those who have not actually seen and sensed the way Hitler reigns over the heart and mind of Germany, this description may appear extravagant. All the same, it is the bare truth."

To reinforce the image of Hitler as the father of his country, Goebbels's efficient propaganda machine afforded generous play to photographs of the unmarried Führer surrounded by adoring youngsters. Although the Nazi press lavished Germans with such comforting icons of their leader, it offered few insights into the man behind the facade—and with good reason. As those who had access to the regime's inner circle knew full well, the magisterial front sustained by Hitler and his top aides covered a multitude of sins and shortcomings. The Führer known to his close associates was far from the omniscient, awe-inspiring figure portrayed to the world. Indeed, this putative master of Europe's destiny was prey to an ominous assortment of private demons.

For years, success had largely glossed over the disturbing flaws in Hitler's character. In the heady spring of 1939, few in the Reich suspected that the man who commanded the new empire was in any way ill suited to the monumental task he had taken on. But soon Hitler would turn his hostile attentions to Poland, launching a war that would test his fiber as never before. Slowly, under the stress of that conflict, the myth of his infallibility would be stripped away, and his privileged paladins would lose their spurious charm and emerge in an unflattering light—as quarrelsome pretenders, more concerned with protecting their own flanks than with guarding their leader's. In the end, the weakened Führer would be caught in a web of intrigue not unlike the ones he had spun to ensnare his enemies in the past. The consummate schemer, Hitler himself would be schemed against—the target of Germans who felt that their country could only be saved by doing away with its misbegotten master.

"Struggle is the father of all things," Hitler once proclaimed from the podium during his arduous ascent to power. "It is not by the principles

of humanity that man lives or is able to preserve himself above the animal world, but solely by means of the most brutal struggle." For Hitler, this view of life as a vicious contest for dominance was not an abstract concept that had been culled from books but a hard lesson literally beaten into him by his overbearing father, Alois, a civil servant who died when Hitler was thirteen. In *Mein Kampf*, the testament Hitler dictated to his deputy Hess in the mid-1920s, he portrayed the early conflict with his father as a matter of principle: The old man hoped that his son would follow his example and enter the civil service, while the boy stubbornly held out for a career as an artist. Privately, however, Hitler later admitted that the quarrel had less to do with ideals than with brute intimidation. "I never loved my father," he confessed to one of his secretaries. "He had a terrible temper and often whipped me. My poor mother was always afraid for me." A relative confirmed this grim account, relating that the father would sometimes whip the family dog until it "wet on the floor. He often beat the children and on occasion would beat his wife."

Hitler confided that he had learned to endure such abuse by following the stoic example of the American Indians who populated the stories of Karl May, a German author who wrote fanciful tales about the American West that fascinated youngsters of Hitler's generation. Like the Indian warriors in May's stories, who underwent torture without crying out, Adolf silently absorbed repeated blows from his father's cane, then proudly reported the exact number of strokes to his mother. (Grateful for such inspiration, the adult Hitler remained devoted to May's fiction; he kept the author's complete works, bound in vellum, on a large shelf in his Berlin library, consulting them for insights about life in America and even recommending them to his generals as morale boosters.)

If Hitler was ashamed of his father's brutality, he was nonetheless proud of his own ability as a youth to withstand the punishment—a quality he demonstrated again as a soldier, wounded twice on the western front, and later as a Nazi firebrand, campaigning to the limits of human endurance. And as he rose to power, Hitler tacitly endorsed his father's intimidating lesson—and expanded on it—by instituting a policy of terror aimed at eliminating the party's most determined opponents and reducing the rest to childlike submissiveness.

Alois Hitler cast another dark cloud over his son's life, one that the Nazi leader was unable to dispel—the mystery of his father's paternity. Alois Hitler was the illegitimate son of an Austrian peasant woman named Maria Schickelgruber, who had conceived him while working as a domestic servant in the provincial city of Graz. Although a farmer from the village of Spital, in the parish of Döllersheim, took the boy Alois under his wing and eventually gave him his own name—recorded in the parish register as Hitler—Maria Schickelgruber carried the secret of her son's paternity with her to the grave. Adolf Hitler, try as he might, could never determine the identity of his paternal grandfather, and he never brought the troublesome subject up in conversation.

According to Hans Frank, Hitler's lawyer, the matter came to a head in 1930, when Hitler received a letter from a relative hinting that the mysterious ancestor was a Jew. Fearing that he might be blackmailed, Hitler secretly dispatched Frank on the delicate mission of investigating the charge. Frank returned with information that Hitler's grandmother had been working in the household of a Jewish family named Frankenberger when she became pregnant—and that Herr Frankenberger had paid her support money for fourteen years after she left his employ. Hitler flatly denied that the payments were any indication of paternity, telling Frank that his grandmother had once confided to him that she had been forced to accept money from a Jew because she was so poor. This glib response was a patent lie: Maria Schickelgruber had died thirty-five years before Adolf Hitler was born.

Subsequent inquiries turned up no hard evidence to substantiate Frank's alarming report; investigators were unable to document the alleged financial transactions or even to confirm the existence of any Jews named Frankenberger living in Graz. Nevertheless, the possibility that there might indeed be Jewish blood running through his veins evidently tormented Hitler. He flew into a rage when associates so much as mentioned the Austrian village where his father had been raised, and he ordered the removal of a plaque proudly noting that the Führer had spent time there in his youth. He dwelt obsessively on the dangers of racial "pollution" and projected his anxiety by suggesting privately that the population as a whole was tainted. "All of us are suffering from the ailment of mixed, corrupted blood," he once lamented to one of his associates. "How can we purify ourselves and make atonement?"

In 1935, Hitler authorized the inclusion of a revealing clause in the Nuremberg Racial Laws. It stipulated that "Jews cannot employ female household servants of German or related blood who are under forty-five years of age." This noxious provision, which suggested that even women of advanced childbearing age were helpless before the supposed rapacity of Jewish men, seemed designed to prevent any repetition of the scandal Hitler feared in his own family: Maria Schickelgruber had been forty-one years old when she conceived Hitler's father out of wedlock while reportedly serving in a Jewish household.

To be sure, broodings such as these were not the sole cause of Hitler's

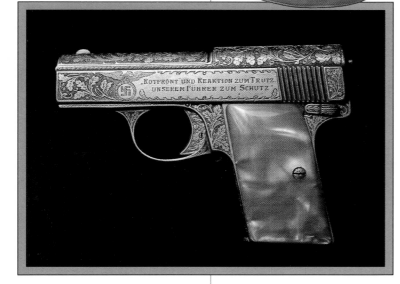

Hitler's austere tunic shows his calculated restraint. Shown just as the Russians found it in 1945, the tunic had no shoulder boards or collar tabs. Hitler also rarely carried a weapon, although he owned this pistol, a gift. Its inscription reads, "In defiance of the Red Front and the Reaction, for the protection of our Führer."

rabid anti-Semitism. Paranoid assumptions about Jews were widespread in his native Austria, and Hitler was influenced by the prevailing climate of bigotry just as he was affected by the crude notions of Social Darwinism, or might makes right, that was often expounded in the street-corner harangues and cheap fiction he reveled in as a young man. What drew millions of followers to him as an adult, however, was not so much the predictable nature of his ideas as the uncanny fervor with which he espoused them—an intensity derived in no small part from his personal history. By transferring his smoldering private resentments to the public arena, he ignited the masses, whose members saw in him the incarnation of their collective hopes and fears.

This ability to whip crowds into a frenzy puzzled those who observed Hitler's phenomenal ascent from a distance. Newsreel viewers around the world saw a ludicrous figure, whose clipped walk and wild gesticulations—both were exaggerated by the choppy film footage of the day—made him seem a kind of posturing Charlie Chaplin caricature, replete with dark toothbrush mustache, that had strutted onto the world's stage to do a quick comic turn. Indeed, the chancellor of Nazi Germany appeared so unlikely a leader that foreign political analysts searched doggedly for signs of a power working behind the throne—a master politician or wily industrialist who was quietly pulling the puppet's strings. As one American journalist described it, the baffled pundits came to agree that "some stronger man must be behind a leader who looks like Adolf Hitler."

Those who surrounded Hitler and dealt with him on a daily basis were similarly struck by the less-than-imposing figure he cut—an apparent

contradiction, given the inordinate emphasis the Führer himself placed on noble proportions as a yardstick of racial worth. Barely five feet nine inches tall, with wide hips and thin, short legs, Hitler could not have met the entrance requirements of his own elite guard. Yet as awkward as he appeared, few who spent any time around Hitler failed to sense the pull of a personal magnetism that defied rational analysis. Its power emanated from his one truly remarkable physical characteristic—his pale blue eyes, whose searching glance became the stuff of legend in Nazi Germany. Party lore was rife with testimony to the riveting effect of those eyes. One tale told of an anti-Nazi police officer assigned to control the crowd at an early Hitler rally; the man was so affected by a single transfixing look from the Führer

Seated beside Magda and Joseph Goebbels at a garden party thrown in Berlin, Hitler fixes his riveting stare on a guest. One ardent admirer wrote to the Führer, "It is as if your eyes were equipped with hands, for they grip a man and hold him fast."

that he promptly joined the party. The German dramatist Gerhart Hauptmann reverently described his first gaze into the Führer's eyes as the "greatest moment of my life."

Hitler's penetrating glance, combined with his insistent manner of speaking, mesmerized battle-hardened commanders as well as fawning party functionaries. Even Hermann Göring, one of the proudest and most powerful men in the Reich, lost his self-possession in Hitler's presence. Hitler was acutely aware of his ability to sweep people off their feet. And he freely admitted that his dazzling performances, whether before a few listeners or before thousands, were not entirely spontaneous but involved considerable calculation. He once boasted that he was "Europe's greatest actor." A man who so ruthlessly repressed his natural responses in daily life that he seldom laughed without concealing his mouth behind his hand, he mastered an impressive repertoire of movements and poses that lent a powerful intensity to his utterances. Convinced, as he put it in *Mein Kampf,* that "all great, world-shaking events have been brought about not by written matter, but by the spoken word," he constantly refined his stagecraft until he was "practiced in the pathos and gestures that a great hall, with its thousands of people, demands." Nor was his success in the limelight simply a matter of technique; Hitler threw himself into his part with such ardor that he lent the ring of conviction to the baldest lies.

The object of this consummate showmanship was not to convince listeners but to overwhelm them. Hitler recognized that many of his potential followers were haunted by a sense of inadequacy and alienation and that the best way to reach such disaffected citizens was to immerse them in a cauldron of humanity and stir the mass to a peak of excitement. As Hitler noted in *Mein Kampf,* such a ritual enabled the man who "feels very small" to enter into something larger and more powerful: "He is swept away by three or four thousand others into the mighty effect of suggestive intoxication and enthusiasm." A doctrine drummed into an audience in this state would remain fixed in the listeners' minds, Hitler believed, because it carried the hypnotic power of "mass suggestion."

Hitler left nothing to chance in ensuring a receptive attitude among his subjects when he mounted the podium to speak at the mass rallies that secured his hold on the public. He scheduled his speeches after dark, when he could employ dramatic lighting and his listeners would be more impressionable. "At night," he said, "they succumb more easily to the dominating force of a stronger will." To render the crowd all the more susceptible, rally organizers employed huge backdrops, fanfares, and costumed ranks of supporters whose rigid bearing told of their unswerving commitment to the Führer.

The French ambassador, André François-Poncet, described a large rally at Berlin's Tempelhof airfield not long after Hitler had taken power: "At dusk, the streets of Berlin were packed with wide columns of men headed for the rally, marching behind banners, with fife-and-drum units and regimental bands in attendance." Lured by these strutting pied pipers, the masses flocked to the festival. Soon nearly a million eager civilians jammed the field, assembled behind military units and black-suited SS guards. Above the "forest of glittering banners," François-Poncet reported, "a grandstand bristling with microphones cut forward like a prow looming over a sea of human heads."

Various Nazi leaders preceded Hitler at the lectern, fanning the enthusiasm of the crowd until finally, at eight o'clock, the Führer arrived. "Hitler made his appearance, standing in his car, his arm outstretched, his face stern and drawn. A protracted clamor of powerful acclaim greeted his passage. Night was now fallen. Floodlights were turned on, set at spacious

gaps, their gentle bluish light allowing for dark, intervening spaces. The perspective of this human sea stretched out to infinity." As Hitler took the stand, François-Poncet noted, "all the floodlights were turned off save such as might envelop the Führer in so dazzling a nimbus that he seemed to be looming upon that magical prow over the human tide below. The crowd lapsed into a religious silence."

The buildup was breathtaking, but the first several minutes of the oration were anticlimactic. Hitler fumbled for his opening words and spoke haltingly in harsh gutteral tones. Then, as he warmed to his theme, he became more fluent. "After fifteen minutes," one observer remarked, "something occurs that can only be described by the ancient, primitive metaphor: The spirit enters into him." The voice grew steadily louder, the tempo faster. Perspiration started to stream down Hitler's face, and all the emotion he suppressed in daily life rose to the surface as he engaged his audience with an intensity that he never allowed himself in ordinary discourse. Eyes glazed, he looked hypnotized.

It was his listeners, however, who were spellbound. Whenever Hitler swayed from side to side, the audience swayed as one along with him; when he leaned forward, the crowd surged toward him like a wave. Inflamed by his rhetorical raptures, women shrieked and fainted. Even determined skeptics, including neutral diplomats and foreign journalists, found themselves spontaneously shooting out their arms in stiff salutes and shouting, *Sieg heil!*

As Hitler's oratorical passion reached its peak, he scowled in anger and brandished his fists as if he were in the very presence of his appointed enemies: the Jews, the Reds, the hated appeasers who had betrayed Germany to the foe and reduced the nation to near impotence. His language grew visceral—filled with images of blood and violation, delivered in tones both cruel and confiding. His lurid verbal assaults lashed the audience into a paroxysm that raged on after his tirade was done. Goebbels reported gleefully after one such speech in Berlin: "The Sportpalast roared and raved for a whole hour in a delirium of unconsciousness." Hitler himself would stand dazed and spent, soaking wet. (He once confided that he perspired so heavily while delivering his speeches that during each one he lost four to six pounds in weight.)

Those who attempted to analyze the shattering power of Hitler's oratory and convey its effect often resorted to sexual metaphors. "In his speeches we hear the suppressed voice of passion and wooing, which is taken from the language of love," observed Axel Heyst, a Polish correspondent. "He utters a cry of hate and voluptuousness, a spasm of violence and cruelty. All those tones and sounds are taken from the back streets of the instincts;

Conditioned by their elders, children squeeze past smiling SS guards to offer the Nazi salute at a party rally. German educators, operating on Hitler's premise that "the masses are like an animal that obeys its instincts," required pupils to render the stiff-armed salute—and the words "Heil Hitler!"—dozens of times each day, hoping that it would instill an unthinking devotion to the regime.

they remind us of dark impulses repressed too long." The poet René Schickele described the dramatic effect of Hitler's oratory more succinctly, branding it "rape and murder."

Much of what Hitler himself said about his own performances bore out the sexual interpretations. He often characterized the masses as feminine in nature and took unconcealed pride in his ability to manipulate them. In *Mein Kampf*, he noted provocatively that "the psyche of the broad masses does not respond to anything weak or halfway. Like a woman, whose spiritual sensitiveness is determined less by abstract reason than by an indefinable emotional longing for fulfilling power, and who for that reason prefers to submit to the strong rather than the weakling—the mass, too, prefers the ruler to a pleader."

In order to maintain the upper hand in this coercive relationship, Hitler did his best to prevent the adoring public from learning much about him. Only a few of his trusted intimates could appreciate the extent to which Hitler's masterful pose concealed his private deficiencies. And as these witnesses later revealed, behind the leader's spellbinding mask hid a flawed and vulnerable figure.

Among the curious secrets harbored by those who frequented Hitler's inner circle was that the all-powerful Führer took little interest in running the country. Despite his keen political instincts, he had only a dim understanding of the day-to-day workings of government and made no attempt to learn more; administration simply did not fit his exalted image of himself as an artist and inspired thinker. "A single idea of genius is worth more than a lifetime of continuous office work," he declared jauntily, and he governed by this axiom, frittering away his days until inspiration or crisis would ignite a burst of feverish activity.

The pattern held even when Hitler was settled in the Reich Chancellery in Berlin, his seat of power. Typically, he rose late, read the newspapers while nibbling a Spartan breakfast, then repaired to his office to attend to those matters that interested him and to avoid all else. He made up his own appointments list, and officials he did not want to see would not be admitted—no matter how pressing their business. He rarely sat at his imposing desk, preferring to pace around the office. Rather than issue an order in writing, he would bark a directive at whoever happened to be standing nearby, with the understanding that the command would be passed on to the appropriate official.

The highlight of the day was lunch in the Chancellery dining room. The guests—any number of a group of some fifty cronies, who needed only to phone ahead to have a place set for them—gathered in the spacious

An orator almost without equal, Hitler reinforced his arguments with an array of rehearsed gestures, as these photographs by Heinrich Hoffmann show. Unlike Churchill and Roosevelt, who mastered the medium of radio, Hitler preferred a large, live audience. "I must have a crowd when I speak," he said.

entrance hall, a tapestry-lined room with dark red marble floors. There they lingered for a while (it was the only room in which the abstemious Hitler permitted smoking) before moving into the living room, where they awaited their leader. Lunch was usually set for two o'clock, but it was rarely served until after three, when the Führer, who disdained punctuality, arrived and led the way through a glass door into the breezy dining hall, which overlooked a pleasant garden.

The party arranged itself around a large center table seating fifteen; any overflow guests took their places at smaller tables in the corners. Then waiters brought out a simple meal while Hitler launched into the inevitable prolix monologue that took the place of genuine conversation at his table. For an hour or two, Hitler would air his views on history, architecture, painting, diet, or one of his other pet concerns. He would talk about his dogs and about the early glory days of his Nazi party, about movies and operettas and their stars, about other people's troubled family lives. He rarely solicited the opinions of his guests, and anyone who attempted to move the discourse beyond simple expressions of agreement risked a blistering rebuff. First-timers went slack-jawed at the torrent of words; hardened veterans gritted their teeth and struggled to conceal their boredom. "The repertory remained the same," complained Albert Speer, a bright young architect whom Hitler took under his wing in 1933. "He neither extended nor deepened it, scarcely ever enriched it by new approaches. He did not even try to cover up the frequent repetitions. I cannot say I found his remarks very impressive."

Speer did not find the company very impressive either. For the most part, the luncheon crowd was made up of Nazi party flunkies and provincial administrators—"almost to a man without cosmopolitan experience," sniffed Speer, himself the product of an upper-class background. In the evenings, a smaller but no more distinguished circle gathered around the Führer for dinner. This entourage included his bodyguards, pilot, chauffeur, and two doctors; his official photographer, Heinrich Hoffmann; his administrative secretary, Martin Bormann; and a handful of military adjutants. Among the regime's leading figures, only Goebbels spent much time with Hitler at the Reich Chancellery. Himmler and Göring rarely put in an appearance, and high-ranking military officers made themselves similarly scarce. Understandably, proud men found it difficult to pay court to Hitler. And he, in turn, preferred the company of unassuming personalities, perhaps sensing that those who were constantly in his presence were bound to build up some immunity to his vaunted charisma; only self-effacing figures could be counted on to lose that worshipful attitude and still hang on his every word.

Hitler returns the crowd's salute in January 1938, on the fifth anniversary of the Nazi takeover. Seeking a proper stage for such appearances, the Führer had a balcony added to the old chancellery in Berlin soon after he took power. He provided his architect, Albert Speer, with a plan he drew himself (*inset*).

In a typical monologue, Hitler holds forth to an audience of sycophants, including Deputy Führer Hess (*at center, with arms folded*).

An aide complained that Hitler "spoke incessantly, not giving anyone a chance to interject more than a comment now and then."

A day at the Reich Chancellery usually ended with the showing of films—the only form of entertainment that the reclusive Hitler indulged in regularly. Several movies were stockpiled for each showing, allowing the Führer to exercise his options. Regardless of what his guests thought of a film, when he became bored he shouted, "Trash!" and the projectionist obediently went on to the next feature. Hitler was fond of French films—although he refused to allow the German public to view them—and he doted on light American fare, such as *Snow White and the Seven Dwarfs*. One of his favorite features was *Lives of a Bengal Lancer*. As a British diplomat who visited the Berlin Chancellery explained, "He liked this film because it depicted a handful of Britons holding a continent in thrall. That was how a superior race must behave."

Matters of state seldom kept Hitler in the capital city for long. He was constantly on the move, traveling around Germany with his entourage in his private plane, by special train, or in a fleet of Mercedes-Benz motorcars. The Führer felt most at home in Bavaria, the region that had nurtured him from anonymity to notoriety in the years after World War I. Whenever possible, he would spend a few days at his Munich apartment. While there, he haunted the local cafés, treating members of his retinue to his thoughts in between bites of the sweet pastries he craved. Then he would repair to his Alpine retreat near the town of Berchtesgaden. His estate there, purchased with royalties garnered from the sales of *Mein Kampf* before he came to power, consisted originally of a modest mountainside lodge surrounded by pine forests. Footpaths that laced the woods offered Hitler a rare chance to roam at will.

In the mid-1930s, however, the place was transformed into a closed compound that was ringed by barbed-wire fences and watched over by armed detachments. The original lodge was subsumed within a multistory chalet, whose lower floors were recessed deep into the mountain to accommodate kitchens, food cellars, guardrooms, and other chambers. Above this comfortable residence, known as the Berghof, stood the so-called Eagle's Nest, an isolated mountaintop teahouse reached by an elevator that ran up through the cliff. This well-furnished perch was conceived as a meditation chamber where Hitler could ponder his grand schemes, but he seldom visited it; he preferred to do his brooding in the living room of the Berghof, whose broad picture window offered a sweeping view of the Austrian frontier.

As Speer remarked, the transformation of Hitler's rustic Alpine lodge into a forbidding enclosure signaled the dictator's "tendency to withdraw more and more from the wider world around him." Increasingly, he retired to the Berghof for business as well as pleasure. When a major speech loomed,

A constant traveler—although almost all of his touring was within the Reich—Hitler thumbs through a book during a flight *(top)* and studies a map in his open car *(bottom)*, in which he wears aviator's gear to protect against the elements.

Set against the lofty peaks of the Bavarian Alps near Salzburg (*left*), Hitler's villa, the Berghof, provided a comfortable retreat and an ideal setting for him to impress his guests. Below, he leads the Duke and Duchess of Windsor (*to Hitler's right*) on a tour of the grounds in 1937.

he spent days or even weeks there, mulling over its basic themes. He even received foreign emissaries at the chalet, correctly calculating that its lofty isolation would have a chilling effect on those guests he wished to intimidate. But the chief appeal of the place to Hitler was simply the unparalleled privacy it afforded him. He could indulge his whims there without fear of exposure. Significantly, it was at the Berghof that he relinquished the pose of a mysterious bachelor—an image he cultivated to enhance his hold over women in public. Not long after Hitler's official motorcade arrived at the Berghof for one of his frequent stays, a small Mercedes sedan would pull up carrying his mistress, Eva Braun.

This pretty, unpretentious one-time Munich clerk was the quietest of paramours. Visitors at the Berghof who did not know better might well wonder what hold, if any, she had on the Führer, for he seldom showed her much affection in front of others and sometimes treated her with a dismissiveness bordering on contempt. If high-ranking dignitaries showed up to confer with Hitler, she was banished from the table. Once, when the snobbish Hermann Göring and his wife, Emmy, were visiting, Speer found Braun cowering in her bedroom, too intimidated even to step out for a breath of fresh air. "I might meet the Görings in the hall," she whispered. In part, Hitler's distant attitude to her reflected his reluctance to admit that he was intimately tied to anyone—let alone a woman of such common breeding. But their relationship was complicated by another unsettling factor—the memory of the young woman who had preceded Braun in Hitler's affections: his niece, Geli Raubal.

Hitler had first fallen under Raubal's spell at his lodge near Berchtesgaden in 1928, when he summoned his half sister, Angela, to serve as housekeeper there. Angela brought along her two daughters, Friedl and the fetching Geli, who at the age of twenty was nineteen years Hitler's junior. Hitler kept Geli close throughout the next few years, doting on her with a passion that was apparently never consummated. As one associate recalled, "To him, she was the personification of perfect young womanhood—beautiful, fresh, and unspoiled." Ultimately, Hitler's insistence on controlling Raubal's every movement drove her to despair. In September of 1931, she was found dead in his Munich apartment with a bullet through her heart, an apparent suicide.

The event devastated Hitler. Although he soon sought consolation in the company of Braun—whom he had first met in 1930 in the shop of his photographer, Hoffmann—Raubal remained a hallowed figure for Hitler. Braun herself seemed painfully aware of Raubal's posthumous hold on Hitler and made a desperate bid to emulate her: In 1932, she shot herself in the chest, barely missing her heart. Three years later, she made a second unsuccessful suicide attempt, this time with pills. Thereafter, Hitler adopted a more protective attitude toward her in private but confined their liaisons to Munich or the Berghof. Raubal, inviolate in his memory, was the only woman other than his mother that he ever admitted loving. Braun, whose bedroom adjoined Hitler's in the Berghof, paid a price for that intimacy by existing there as a marginal and somewhat shameful presence, referred to obliquely by the servants as "E.B." Hitler once remarked to others in her presence that a man of high intelligence should take up with a "primitive and stupid woman," one who could be trusted not to interfere in his work. "I could never marry," he added emphatically. "Think of the problems if I had children!"

Eva Braun was not the only member of Hitler's entourage who learned the limits of his affections the hard way. Flattered by his occasional confidences, several of the men around Hitler aspired to the status of true friend to the Führer, only to come up against an unyielding emotional barrier. Albert Speer sometimes found himself asking: "Why can't I call Hitler my friend? What is missing?" The architect eventually concluded that "everything was missing. Never in my life have I met a person who so seldom revealed his feelings and, if he did so, instantly locked them away again." In fact, Hitler often commented that aside from Braun and his dog—two creatures on whose devotion he could always count—he would have no other friends.

If Hitler seldom allowed his acquaintances to feel truly close to him, he did permit them the enjoyment of a few modest liberties. Privileged guests at the Berghof greeted one another with a simple *Guten Tag!*—Good day—instead of the ubiquitous salute, "Heil Hitler!" In addition, they were allowed to refer to their host as "Chief" rather than *mein Führer.* Braun could get away with pointing out to the dowdy dictator that his tie did not go with his suit. And in her daring moments, she might even joke that she was "mother of the country."

This shallow vein of informality did little to lessen the tedium of life at the Berghof, however. The routine there resembled the stultifying one at the Reich Chancellery in Berlin, except that the guests were captive to their

A tame jackdaw perches on the Führer's shoulder in one of the few photographs he allowed that portrayed him in a slightly frivolous way. As a rule, Hitler enjoyed a laugh only when the joke was on someone else.

talkative host not for hours but for days on end. Outsiders often told Otto Dietrich, the Nazi press secretary, how they envied him for being in Hitler's presence all the time. But those who actually received an invitation to join the Führer at the Berghof, Dietrich noted, usually left breathing a massive sigh of relief and expressing pity for the unfortunates "who had to give up their private lives and spend all their time in the nerve-racking atmosphere that Hitler engendered."

It was not just Hitler's tedious monologues that strained the nerves of his guests. In many ways, spending time under Hitler's roof was like living with a particularly immature and trying adolescent. His eating habits were those of a finicky child. He gobbled sweets by the boxful and ladled several teaspoons of sugar into every cup. Nonetheless, he not only refused to eat meat but made a fetish of his vegetarianism, launching into nauseating descriptions of the slaughterhouse just as his hungry guests were tucking into their roasts or porkchops.

Though noted for his lack of humor, Hitler loved practical jokes at others' expense. A favorite form of ribbing was to have one subordinate phone another with intimidating "Führer orders" as Hitler hovered nearby, relishing the thought of the frightened reaction at the other end of the line. He also delighted in witless games, such as a form of bowling he invented: He took the first turn and tried to knock down all the pins with three balls. If he succeeded, another guest could go; if he failed, the game was over. And he liked to see how fast he could dress or undress himself, stationing his valet—who was not allowed to see him unclothed—outside the bedroom door with a stopwatch. The valet would cry, *Los!* and Hitler would scramble into his clothes; when he was done, Hitler would shout, *Schluss!* to stop the timer, then dash to the door to see if he had broken his record.

Despite the patent silliness of some of his behavior, Hitler dreaded appearing ridiculous. Obsessed with his image, he would never be seen in public in a new piece of clothing unless Hoffmann had first photographed him wearing it so he could see how he looked. "The fear of being ridiculed became almost a sickness with him," said one of his secretaries, Christa Schroeder, who would sometimes covertly watch the Führer playing affectionately with his Scottish terrier, Burli. The minute Hitler noticed her, he would chase the little dog away—only to call it back with tender words as soon as Schroeder left the room. Hoffmann was strictly forbidden to release any photographs of the Führer with Burli; Hitler consented to be pictured as a dog lover only after Martin Bormann presented him with a stately Alsatian named Blondi. "In all seriousness," Schroeder recalled later, "he declared that a man in his position could only show himself in public with a German shepherd."

Hitler's tenderness toward animals was at bizarre odds with his ghoulish interest in any form of human torture—the more gruesome the better. He reveled in discussions of dismemberment and decapitation, of bloodletting and cannibalism. (Asked what he would do when he first set foot in England, he replied that he would visit the Tower of London and see where Henry VIII had chopped off his wives' heads.) Yet he fretted endlessly over the mistreatment of pets and drafted elaborate laws governing their care. In 1936, after worried research and debate, he decided the most humane way to kill a lobster was to plunge it into boiling water—and he decreed that henceforth that was how all crustaceans were to be dispatched.

Hitler's strict vegetarianism, however, sprang less from his concern for animals than from his obsession with his health. He was a hypochondriac who abhorred alcohol, never smoked, and kept his doctors, Karl Brandt and Theodor Morell, with him most of the time. They found him a difficult patient who hated to have his body examined and questioned them minutely and mistrustfully about their remedies, fueling his inquiries with information gleaned from a thick, well-thumbed medical text and from his library of pseudoscientific literature.

Dr. Morell—who soon overshadowed Brandt—won Hitler's gratitude in 1936 by treating him for severe stomach cramps, a condition likely aggravated by his peculiar diet and persistent anxiety. Morell prescribed Mutaflor, a supposedly beneficial strain of bacteria, and the cure worked. Hitler put on weight, and a stubborn case of eczema on his leg mysteriously

Fearing for his health, Hitler penned this will in May of 1938. The first clause specifies that his body be taken to Munich and displayed at the Feldherrnhalle, a shrine honoring the Nazi party's first martyrs. The second clause designates the party as the Führer's beneficiary.

cleared up. Delighted, Hitler became increasingly dependent on the doctor, whose regimen involved frequent doses of hormones and other potentially harmful substances. When the Führer complained of flatulence, for example, Morell prescribed pills that contained tiny amounts of strychnine. Some in Hitler's circle considered Morell a dangerous quack, but the Führer stayed with him even though his digestive problems eventually returned with a vengeance and his other assorted complaints—including chronic insomnia—showed no signs of abating. Once, when Hitler seemed reluctant to submit himself to a new treatment Morell was proposing, the doctor reprimanded him: "Mein Führer, I have taken on the responsibility to protect your health. What if something should happen to you?" Hitler clenched his fist menacingly and replied, "Morell, if something should happen to me, your life would be worth nothing."

One of Hitler's persistent anxieties was that he would be stricken by cancer—the disease that had killed his mother—and die before his great plans for Germany were realized. Frequently hoarse from his long speeches, he became convinced that he was suffering from throat cancer. The dread persisted even after he underwent an examination by a throat specialist, who removed a benign polyp from his larynx. In May 1938, Hitler scrawled his will, assuring associates he would not live much longer. Such morbid interludes led him to push for hasty execution of his plans of conquest and to dismiss with contempt anyone who counseled caution.

Hitler's medical fears and fetishes contrasted sharply with his image of himself as a supremely rational man, free of mystic compulsions. In truth, like many of his prominent followers, he often confused superstition with science. Among his enthusiasms was the discredited theory of phrenology, which held that a person's character and capacities could be analyzed in detail by studying the shape of his or her skull. At one point, Hitler summoned experts to take careful measurements of his cranium and then had the dimensions compared with those derived from death masks and portraits of other famous leaders. Predictably, the authorities were happy to confirm that Hitler's cranium shared key characteristics with those of Napoléon, Frederick the Great, and Bismarck.

Indeed, nearly everyone who dealt with Hitler was happy to confirm what the leader wanted to hear because his rages were famous—both for their intensity and for their terrifying unpredictability. Visitors and intimates alike were often dumbfounded by his sudden transformation from a genial host into a howling fury: He screamed, beat his fists on the table, or dramatically spread himself against a wall as if crucified. Sometimes Hitler staged such fits of anger to frighten opponents of his policies into line. In other instances, however, he flew into genuine tantrums, provoked by the most trivial incidents.

One day, when a large group of Hitler's admirers were admitted to the Berchtesgaden estate to pay homage to the Führer, his dog Blondi unaccountably failed to come to heel when Hitler ordered. Otto Dietrich witnessed the Führer's reaction. "I saw the blood rush to his head at this defiance of his command," he wrote. "There was a crowd of several thousand people around, and Hitler was about to take his customary walk past these visitors. Two minutes later, when a woman handed him a petition, he suddenly screamed at one of his closest associates, who happened to be standing behind him. Without giving any explanation, disregarding the amazement of the crowd, he gave the man a ferocious bawling out over nothing." But this tantrum was mild compared with that directed at Karl Wilhelm Krause, an orderly, who served Hitler spring water one day instead of the Führer's favorite bottled mineral water. After five years as Hitler's trusted companion, Krause was fired on the spot.

The more perceptive of Hitler's acquaintances sensed that these startling, childlike outbursts welled up from some seething source of resentment that was lodged deep in his past. "What a vain and touchy creature the man must have been in his obscure youth!" reflected one guest after witnessing a sudden demonstration of Hitler's anger. "In some hapless remark, the visitor will have unwittingly touched one of the leader's sore points, reopened some wound to his self-confidence and vanity." Christa Schroeder, one of the few who ever heard Hitler speak of his father's brutality, speculated that her boss's volatile personality was a product of his "joyless childhood." That a man of such unbridled authority might be fundamentally unbalanced was not an insight that those around him cared to dwell on, however. Instead, they did their best to humor him and to sweep his embarrassing lapses under the rug. As a result, this ominous figure, whom even his own press secretary characterized as "often brutal, inflexible, senselessly furious," continued to be revered by millions as the kindly father of his people.

Hitler put the best face on his peculiar temperament and unorthodox lifestyle by referring to himself repeatedly as an artist, exempt from normal standards by virtue of his genius. To back up that claim, he could point not only to his extraordinary rhetorical gift but to his phenomenal will power and his uncanny sense of timing. Though not a learned man, he had a keen eye for detail and a superb memory, which enabled him to master diplomatic and military fine points and avoid the dependence on advisers that reduced lesser statesmen to mere caretakers. For all his apparent procrastination, he was a virtuoso at orchestrating events, lulling opponents into a false sense of security and then overwhelming them with a furious burst of activity. Like an artist brazenly defying the conventions of his times, he pursued his bold vision of a new European order with utter disdain for the critics. Those skeptics in the army who sensed folly in his plans for German expansion were maneuvered out of the way, and the naysayers abroad—who dismissed Hitler as a rank amateur on the world stage and prophesied his imminent fall—were forced to eat their words.

Yet Adolf Hitler's initial success in achieving his grand designs exacted a steep price. In the late 1930s, as events seemed to confirm his brilliance, he assumed a kind of divine infallibility, portraying himself as the agent of God and the vehicle of providence. For some time already, Nazi educators and journalists had been using similar language to tout Hitler as the nation's savior; German children regularly recited a prayer that began, "Führer, my Führer, bequeathed to me by the Lord." Now, however, the idolatry went to Hitler's head.

In April of 1938, he appeared before an adoring crowd in recently annexed Austria as a heaven-sent redeemer. "I believe that it was God's will to send a youth from here into the Reich," he averred, "to let him grow up, to raise him to be the leader of the nation so as to enable him to lead his homeland back into the Reich." Hitler's growing conviction that he was carrying out an ordained plan only increased his sense of isolation and stiffened his resistance to criticism. Surrounded by worshipful acolytes such as Joseph Goebbels, who insisted that "when the Führer speaks it is like a divine service," Hitler came to believe that his inspired judgments were irrefutable. "I go the way that Providence dictates with the assurance of a sleepwalker," he asserted.

Hitler's self-righteous refusal to be guided by any counsel but his own raised deep concern among his generals, who feared that he would lead the army blindly into war before it was prepared for the ordeal. Matters nearly came to a head in the summer of 1938, when Hitler informed his

military chiefs of his intention to invade Czechoslovakia even at the risk of war with the western powers. The announcement prompted a group of senior officers, led by General Franz Halder, chief of the army high command, to speak covertly of removing Hitler from office. The plot dissolved when Britain and France effectively abandoned Czechoslovakia to Germany at Munich in September. Yet resistance to Hitler continued to simmer at high levels within the Wehrmacht. As Chief of Operations Alfred Jodl, a staunch Hitler loyalist, complained: "There is only one undisciplined element in the army—the generals, and in the last analysis this comes from the fact that they are arrogant. They have neither confidence nor discipline because they cannot recognize the Führer's genius."

Recalcitrant officers were not the only ones in Germany who feared the consequences of Hitler's fanatical will. Some members of the diplomatic

Armed with his customary glass of mineral water, Hitler commands the attention of guests at the Führerbau, his Munich headquarters, in early 1939. With unintended irony, he argued that such lavish layouts as the Führerbau and his new Chancellery might help prop up some insecure future leader: "You would hardly believe what power a small mind acquires over the people around him when he is able to show himself in such imposing circumstances."

corps regarded Hitler's aggressive policies not only as dangerous but as dishonorable, since they made Germany a pariah in the international community. For the German diplomat Hans Gisevius, the lawless nature of the regime was shamefully exposed on November 9, 1938, when Nazi mobs burned scores of synagogues across the Reich and ransacked thousands of Jewish-owned stores in an orgy of violence that came to be known as *Kristallnacht*, or the Night of Broken Glass. Gisevius had no illusions as to Hitler's role in the brutal incident. "The Führer himself inaugurated these frightful and portentous excesses," he insisted. Gisevius became an active conspirator against Hitler, hoping to shatter the evil spell that kept the majority of respectable German citizens staring meekly "at the Nazi monster like a rabbit at a snake."

The savagery of Hitler's campaign against the Jews drove other men and women of conscience to seditious thoughts. On learning of *Kristallnacht*, an influential young Lutheran theologian named Dietrich Bonhoeffer opened his Bible to Psalm 74 and wrote the date of that violent outburst— "9.11.38"—next to a verse telling of a sacrilege committed against the ancient Hebrews by the followers of a deranged king: "They burned down every shrine of God in the country." Bonhoeffer took to heart the psalm's call for just retribution against the "madman's daylong blaspheming," and he soon reached the conclusion that it was his religious duty to join those plotting against the regime.

It would be several years, however, before the ill will stirred up by Hitler's hostile maneuvers crystallized into a broad-based conspiracy against him. As war loomed, his real problem was not that he had acquired scattered enemies in high places but that he had failed to surround himself with competent and scrupulous aides. "With his overwhelming need to dominate, Hitler could not permit the development of any other personality," his press chief commented. "Instead of drawing to himself men of high character, rich experience, and breadth of vision, he gave such persons a wide berth and made sure they had no chance to influence him."

In fairness, Hitler's vaunted circle of paladins included a few men of great talent, but their genius was of a narrow kind, constricted by prejudice and vanity or confined to purely technical matters. In the trying years ahead, Hitler would stand in desperate need of wise counsel—advisers who were capable of calming his rising furies and setting him on a safe course whenever he strayed. Instead, the Führer would rely to the bitter end on cronies who shared many of his delusions and who were no better equipped to correct his ways than they were their own. As Otto Dietrich remarked, such was the inevitable fate of an idolized autocrat "who permitted no other gods besides himself." ✚

A Workplace Fit for a Führer

A model of the huge new Reich Chancellery shows the motor entrance on Wilhelmstrasse *(lower right)* that led into the so-called Honor Courtyard. The rest of the block-long building fronted Voss Strasse to the left.

A pair of bronze sculptures representing the Nazi party and the German army, made to Hitler's order by sculptor Arno Breker, flanked the Honor Courtyard's massive entrance to the building. The columns were 42 feet tall, the courtyard 223 feet long.

"I have an urgent assignment for you," Hitler told his favorite architect, Albert Speer, early in 1938. The eighteenth-century building that housed the Nazi government, Hitler complained, was "fit for a soap-company warehouse." He wanted a majestic new chancellery in the heart of Berlin. "Cost is immaterial," he declared. "I shall be holding extremely important conferences in the near future. For these, I need grand halls and salons that will make an impression on people, especially the smaller dignitaries."

As usual, Speer's vision was in harmony with his leader's. He designed a neoclassic structure of intimidating size—a city block long—with imposing marble interiors that satisfied even Hitler's appetite for the grandiose. Employing 4,500 workers night and day in Berlin while several thousand more produced components at distant sites, Speer completed his task in less than one year.

The Reich Chancellery was a series of connected chambers on a long axis. Diplomats and other visitors entered by way of the Honor Courtyard *(right)* and had to hike through four high-ceilinged rooms to reach the inner sanctum. The long walk, chuckled Hitler, gave visitors a proper taste of the "power and grandeur of the German Reich." Color photographs of the chambers are shown in sequence on the following pages. Shaded floor plans give the location of each room, and arrows indicate the points from which the photographs were taken.

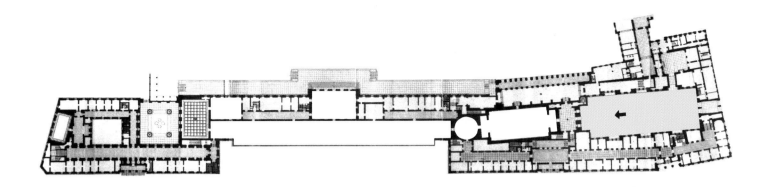

Eagles made of gray marble (*inset*) decorated the walls of the Mosaic Hall, which extended 151 feet to huge mahogany doors.

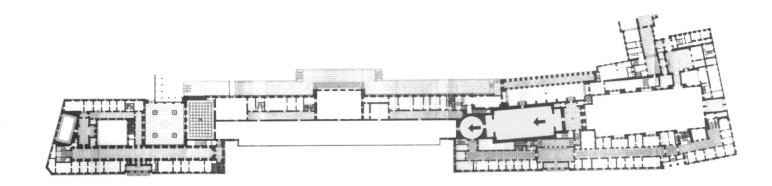

Doors seventeen feet high opened onto the Round Room, which was paved and walled with marble.

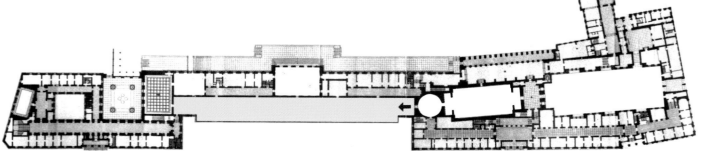

The 480-foot Great Marble Gallery near his office pleased Hitler; it was twice as long as the Hall of Mirrors at Versailles.

Beneath a thirty-two-foot-high ceiling, Hitler's desk had a center inlay of a half-drawn sword. "When diplomats see that," the Führer said, "they'll learn to shiver and shake."

Over the doors opening into Hitler's outsize office, Speer optimistically installed Plato's four Virtues: Wisdom, Fortitude, Temperance, and Justice.

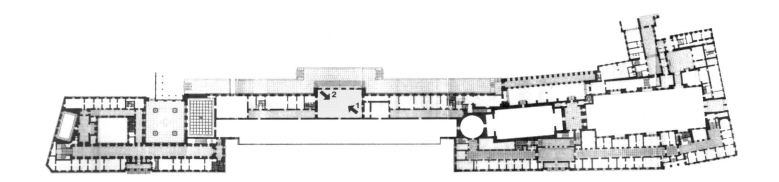

Two dozen Empire chairs, each decorated with the eagle and swastika, ring the Cabinet Room table. Hitler never convened a cabinet

meeting here, but ministers would occasionally come to see their names embossed in gold on the writing pads lying on the table.

The Voracious Lieutenants

Barely six weeks after Hitler's installation as chancellor in January of 1933, Albert Speer received a summons that would lure him irrevocably from the tranquil outskirts of power into the treacherous core of Nazi intrigue. The call reached the twenty-seven-year-old architect at his home in Mannheim, a placid city on the Rhine that was a world apart from the revolutionary tumult in Berlin. Speer had been a registered Nazi since 1931 and dutifully attended local gatherings of the party faithful, but he found the meetings stultifying. "I was struck by the low personal and intellectual level of the members," he recalled. Briefly, a disturbing thought occurred to him: How could a nation be governed by such people? But Speer set aside his misgivings in an instant when Karl Hanke, a rising young Nazi official for whom Speer had performed a few architectural commissions, phoned him with a tempting offer from the capital, where the party's best and brightest were laying the foundations for Hitler's new order. "Would you come to Berlin?" Hanke asked. "There is certainly work for you here." Restless and ambitious, Speer agreed on the spot and left Mannheim with his wife that same evening in their small BMW roadster, driving through the night to reach the capital. Bleary-eyed, he reported directly to Hanke, who put him straight to work. "You're to drive over with the Doctor right away," Hanke instructed. "He wants to have a look at his new ministry."

Speer knew at once whom Hanke was referring to. More than a few Nazis had medical degrees or doctorates, but there was only one "Doctor" in the party pantheon: the minister for popular enlightenment and propaganda, Paul Joseph Goebbels. This thirty-five-year-old prodigy—who stood scarcely five feet tall and limped on a crippled right foot—seemed intent on avenging those slights of nature by casting a giant shadow across Germany. In his new post, he would control the institutions that shaped public opinion in the nation, including the press, radio networks, and filmmaking industry. An erratically brilliant youth, he had studied at eight universities before earning his doctorate in literature. He had then tried his hand without much success as a novelist, poet, playwright, and journalist before finding his niche in the mid-1920s as a publicist for the Nazi party.

As a rousing Nazi orator, he was second only to Hitler, who tolerated a rival in this respect because he knew Goebbels was as loyal as he was gifted. The Führer described him as "my faithful, unshakable shield bearer," and, indeed, of all Hitler's aides, Goebbels came closest to the ideal of the devoted paladin: one ready to lay down his life for his Führer.

Speer had attended a speech delivered by Goebbels in 1931 and had been both fascinated and repelled by the "witch's cauldron of excitement" the little man stirred up. Now he would witness the Doctor's sinister machinations at close quarter. Speer's first assignment was to renovate the stately building on Berlin's Wilhelmplatz that Goebbels had requisitioned as his Propaganda Ministry. "He gave me a formal assignment to begin at once," Speer noted, "without waiting for an estimate of costs and without troubling to find out whether funds were available." As Speer soon discovered, such spendthrift ways were common among Hitler's top aides, who were accountable to no one but the similarly prodigal Führer. Given carte blanche, Speer exercised a certain restraint, refurbishing the building in a manner that respected its original design and avoided excessive ornamentation. The result almost ended Speer's career as a Nazi architect before it had properly begun. After several months of work and considerable expense, Goebbels decided that Speer's plan was "insufficiently impressive" and had the interior redone in a garish fashion that Speer described curtly as "ocean-liner style."

Although Goebbels considered Speer's touch too delicate for his showcase ministry, he was delighted with the work that the young architect performed at his new residence—a home Goebbels had commandeered from a minor cabinet minister before that official even had a chance to resign. Speer undertook to refurbish the residence and attach a large hall to the building in just two months—a rash promise that Goebbels relayed to an incredulous Hitler. Informed of the Führer's doubts, Speer kept three shifts at work around the clock and completed the project within the deadline. Then, to top off his work, he "borrowed" some watercolors by the German expressionist Emil Nolde from the Berlin National Gallery and hung them in the residence. Goebbels and his wife, Magda, were enchanted by the pictures. But when Hitler toured the house, he was outraged to see modern art on display. As he had enunciated in *Mein Kampf*—a dense tome that Speer, for one, could never plow through—such avant-garde works were the cultural equivalent of bolshevism. Hitler scolded Goebbels, who berated the architect: "The pictures have to go at once; they're simply impossible!" It was Speer's first glimpse of Hitler's capacity to bend his proud subordinates to his will. "Goebbels had simply groveled before Hitler," Speer remarked. "We were all in the same boat. I, too, though alto-

The Hub of Nazi Power

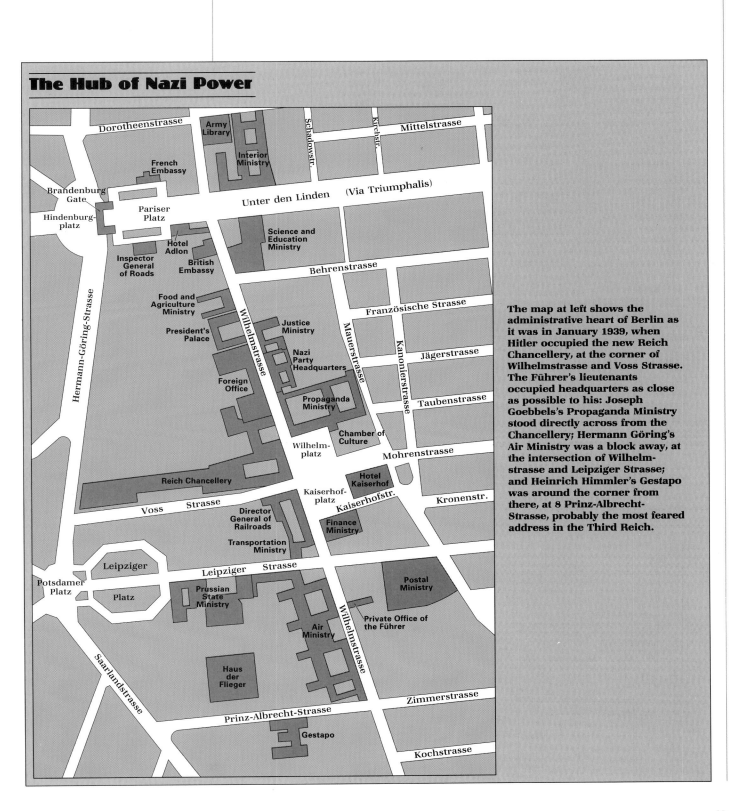

The map at left shows the administrative heart of Berlin as it was in January 1939, when Hitler occupied the new Reich Chancellery, at the corner of Wilhelmstrasse and Voss Strasse. The Führer's lieutenants occupied headquarters as close as possible to his: Joseph Goebbels's Propaganda Ministry stood directly across from the Chancellery; Hermann Göring's Air Ministry was a block away, at the intersection of Wilhelmstrasse and Leipziger Strasse; and Heinrich Himmler's Gestapo was around the corner from there, at 8 Prinz-Albrecht-Strasse, probably the most feared address in the Third Reich.

gether at home in modern art, tacitly accepted Hitler's pronouncement."

Speer soon had occasion to witness such kowtowing on a larger scale. Despite Speer's artistic gaffe, Hitler admired the sheer efficiency of his work for Goebbels and took the architect in tow. Before long, the newcomer was a regular guest at Hitler's table, drawing envious looks from the Führer's longtime cronies. Among those who cast a jaundiced eye on Speer was a man who had reason to consider himself Hitler's leading lieutenant, Hermann Göring. A flamboyant figure whose expanding girth and love of pomp made him a popular foil for the spare and reclusive Hitler, Göring was at heart a cunning predator. A celebrated fighter pilot in the world war, he had joined forces with Hitler in 1922, at the age of twenty-nine, serving initially as commander of the party's notorious Storm Troopers, or Brownshirts, assigned to intimidate opponents. As Göring explained, he threw his lot with the Nazis because he wanted to take part in a revolution, "not because of any ideological nonsense." As Hitler rose to power, Göring

Hitler reviews a building plan with Albert Speer at the Berghof in 1934. Flattered by the Führer's interest in his work, the young architect found himself "completely under Hitler's spell. I was ready to follow him anywhere."

seized control of Prussia, Germany's largest state, and forged the dreaded political police force there known as the Gestapo. Soon he would turn his energies to the rebirth of the German air force, a herculean effort that would solidify his position as the second most powerful man in the Reich.

If any of Hitler's aides had the stature to stand up to the Führer, it was Göring. Yet, as Speer discovered, Göring acted more like a peon than a prince in Hitler's presence. Around the time that Speer was working on Goebbels's home, Göring had his own Berlin residence redone at great expense, siphoning the funds from the Prussian treasury. A pretentious and gloomy building emerged, in which curtains of thick velvet covered stained-glass windows. When Hitler toured the place, he dismissed it with words that mortified Göring. "Dark!" he exclaimed. "How can anyone live in such darkness?" A few months later, still smarting from the rebuff, Göring was dining with Hitler and Speer when he hit on a way of regaining the Führer's aesthetic approval while asserting some authority over the architect. "Is Speer doing your residence, mein Führer?" Göring asked. "Is he your architect?" Speer was not yet serving in that capacity, but as if to goad Göring, Hitler answered in the affirmative. "Then permit me to have him remodel my house, too," Göring ventured. Hitler agreed, and as soon as the meal ended, Göring hustled Speer into his limousine and whisked him away, as the architect put it, "like a piece of booty."

Arriving at Göring's residence, Speer found that it more than lived up to its dismal billing. The rooms were small and dreary and crowded with bulky antiques. "There was a kind of chapel presided over by the swastika," Speer noted, "and the new symbol had also been reiterated on ceilings, walls, and floors throughout the house. There was the feeling that something terribly solemn and tragic would always be going on in this place." Göring made no attempt to defend the decor. "I can't stand it myself," he insisted to Speer. "Do it any way you like. I'm giving you a free hand—only it must turn out like the Führer's place."

Lavishly armed with state funds, Speer had workers tear down walls to create spacious chambers for Göring, including a 1,500-square-foot study that was nearly as large as Hitler's office. To shed some light on the funereal residence, Speer constructed an annex with glass panels framed in bronze—a metal restricted in Germany to vital military and industrial applications, but one that Göring had no difficulty procuring for his private use. The building's main hall displayed a masterwork that Hitler could scarcely object to—Rubens's *Diana at the Stag Hunt*—which Göring had appropriated from a Berlin museum. (In time, Göring's yen for pilfering great paintings would become a mania.) Yet his prize picture was a huge photograph of Hitler that stood on his desk. The portrait was in fact the

From high above a bonfire ringed by torchbearers, Goebbels addresses the faithful in Berlin's Olympic Stadium during a summer-solstice festival in 1938. The propaganda maestro prided himself on appealing to the "most primitive mass instincts."

standard one that Hitler presented to his top aides, but Göring had his copy blown up to give the impression that he was the Führer's favorite.

While his residence was being redone, Göring stayed in a vacant Berlin mansion whose tasteless decor made his own place look refined. The walls of one room were adorned from top to bottom with gaudy roses in bas-relief—an effect that Speer described as "quintessential atrociousness." Here Speer and Göring conferred frequently with the designer in charge of refurbishing Göring's residence—a cultured gentleman with a discriminating eye. Göring took perverse delight in humiliating the man, pointing to the tacky roses on one occasion and remarking: "Don't you think they're beautiful? I mean to have you decorate all my rooms this way." The man was too intimidated to confess his horror at the idea, and Göring poured it on: "See how wonderfully those roses twine their way up!" Finally, his forehead bathed in sweat, the designer yielded to his tormentor and expressed admiration for the motif. The concession filled Göring with vindictive glee. "They're all like that!" he gloated to Speer afterward. As the architect noted later in his memoirs, Göring's words were all too true. "They were all like that, Göring included," Speer wrote, "for at meals, he now never tired of telling Hitler how bright and expansive his home was now: 'Just like yours, mein Führer.' If Hitler had had roses climbing the walls of his room, Göring would have insisted on roses."

As the episode illustrated, those who toadied to Hitler often sought compensation by exacting the same cringing conformity from their underlings. It was a reflex that stifled criticism not only in minor questions of taste but in vital matters of state and ensured the perpetuation of the brutal biases of the men at the top. Nowhere was this more evident than in the organization hammered together by another of Hitler's obsequious associates: Heinrich Himmler, chief of the SS. As Speer observed, the shadowy Himmler rarely appeared at Hitler's side, choosing to consort with his SS minions, "from whom he could count on unqualified respect." So cowed by his Führer that he was known to click his heels when he talked to Hitler over the phone, Himmler insisted on blind obedience from his own acolytes. Indeed, by imbuing his entire organization with a spirit of unquestioning compliance, Himmler made it into an unparalleled instrument of terror. Secure in the knowledge that his men would carry out any order, however abhorrent, Himmler served energetically as Hitler's deadly enforcer—a fact that helped to explain the tactful distance the two men kept. In 1933, Himmler established the first of the SS concentration camps that would become lasting scars on the Nazi landscape. In 1934, he wrested control of the Gestapo away from Göring and transformed it into a national agency for the surveillance and apprehension of so-called enemies of the state.

At the same time, Himmler indulged his penchant for mysticism by imposing a bizarre set of oaths and rituals on SS recruits in the hope of fostering an elite Aryan brotherhood. Hitler, who was prey to his own superstitions and fancies, regarded Himmler's romantic notions as laughable. "What nonsense!" he scoffed. "Here we have at last reached an age that has left all mysticism behind it, and now he wants to start that all over again. We might just as well have stayed with the Church. At least it had tradition. To think that I may someday be turned into an SS saint!" Yet Hitler never tried to rein in Himmler or cleanse the SS of its mystic streak. Shrewdly, he let his lieutenants have their way within their domains in return for their abject loyalty to him. In Hitler's presence, his top aides were lowly apprentices, but on their own they were sorcerers, reveling in their godlike powers.

Young Speer felt the lure of such intoxicating authority as keenly as any of those around Hitler. Although he had no particular ideological commitment to national socialism, he lent his considerable talents to the planning of its most solemn ceremony—the annual party rally at Nuremberg. Among his innovations was the use of powerful lights to frame the nighttime gatherings on the huge Zeppelin Field there. Over Göring's objections, Speer commandeered 130 antiaircraft searchlights and placed them around the field at intervals of forty feet prior to Hitler's main address. As he recalled proudly, the vertical columns of light "were visible to a height of 20,000 to 25,000 feet, after which they merged into a general glow. The feeling was of a vast room, with the beams serving as mighty pillars of infinitely high outer walls. Now and then a cloud moved through this wreath of lights, bringing an element of surrealistic surprise to the mirage."

For an architect who a few years earlier had been scrounging for minor commissions in Mannheim, the chance to build a "cathedral of light" for the purported savior of Germany and his adoring multitude was worth any sacrifice. Only later did Speer realize the cost of the devil's bargain he had entered into. It was a deal that brought Speer undreamed-of opportunities,

His fists clenched and jaw set, Hermann Göring *(right)* takes an aggressive stance near Hitler during a Nazi street demonstration in 1929. Gratified by Göring's loyalty, Hitler gave him a copy of *Mein Kampf (below);* Göring had the book bound in silver and had his family crest embossed on the clasp.

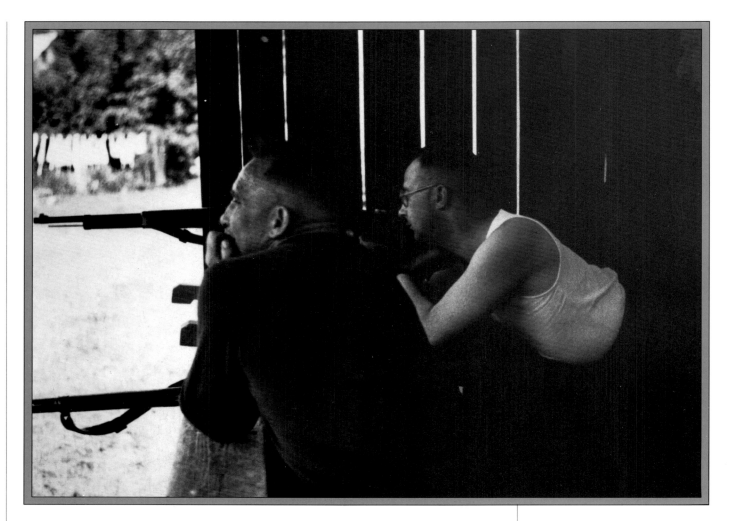

including the chance to rebuild the Reich Chancellery and draw up plans for a new imperial district in Berlin that would form the monumental centerpiece of Hitler's promised 1,000-year Reich. But in the end, Speer became Hitler's creature and assumed a place in his infamous hierarchy.

Speer was something of an exception among Hitler's acolytes in that he had occasional pangs of conscience to contend with and certain principles to betray. Most of the others—including the powerful triumvirate of Goebbels, Göring, and Himmler—were fallen angels from the time they joined the party, unencumbered by scruples. As these ruthless manipulators recognized, the only deadly sin in Hitler's circle was disloyalty to the Führer. All else might be forgiven, and aides made the most of such license by indulging their whims as if Hitler's tenure were one long *Walpurgisnacht*, or May Day's Eve, dreaded by Germans in pagan times as a night when witches and the devil ran loose.

With the possible exception of the venal Hermann Göring, none of Hitler's cronies exploited his connection to the Führer more shamelessly than Julius Streicher, one of the *Alte Kämpfer*, or Old Fighters, who had served Hitler faithfully through the embattled early years of the Nazi movement. Like other ambitious members of that class, Streicher had been rewarded for his efforts with a generous slice of political turf, securing the post of gauleiter, or district leader, for the region of Franconia, in northern Bavaria,

Stripped to his undershirt, SS chieftain Heinrich Himmler takes target practice in 1936. Although Himmler cared little for the human prey tracked down by his national police, he shared Hitler's aversion to the hunting of animals, which he called "pure murder."

a bailiwick that included the party shrine of Nuremberg. Gauleiters were a tough breed who ruled their precincts so haughtily that frustrated party bureaucrats referred to them as "little Hitlers." And Streicher was among the toughest of the lot. Stocky, bull-necked, and bald, he exuded a vitality that captivated his fanatical followers and repelled many other Nazis. He felt free to ignore his critics, for he was the party's foremost exponent of an attitude that was close to Hitler's heart—hatred of the Jews. As early as 1925, Streicher had publicly urged their outright destruction.

The origins of Streicher's fierce anti-Semitism are foggy, although evidence suggests he may have had a Jewish ancestor—a possibility that haunted several high-placed Nazis, including Hitler himself, and sharpened their bigotry. Whatever its source, Streicher's animosity toward the Jews knew no limit. After serving with distinction in World War I, he came home to found a little political party devoted to anti-Semitism. In 1922, at the age of thirty-seven, he took the entire membership with him into Hitler's nascent Nazi movement. The following year, Streicher founded the newspaper *Der Stürmer*, whose fare consisted chiefly of scurrilous articles and cartoons that held Jews responsible for an outlandish assortment of evils, ranging from the betrayal of Germany to the Allies at the end of the Great War to the seduction of Aryan virgins, a threat that Streicher's rag spelled out in pornographic detail.

Hitler loved *Der Stürmer*, remarking that it was the only newspaper he read from front to back. And he so admired the energy and loyalty of its editor that for a long time Streicher was one of the handful of men the Führer addressed in friendly fashion as *du* (you) instead of formally as *Sie*. Streicher, for his part, never forgot his reaction when he first heard Hitler speak: Like the man sitting next to him in the beer hall, he was convinced he could see a halo around Hitler's head. Aside from his labors for *Der Stürmer*, which reached a peak circulation of 700,000 in the late 1930s, and his duties as gauleiter of Franconia, Streicher served as Hitler's point man on race. The Führer selected him to direct one of the regime's first overt acts of anti-Semitism, the boycott of Jewish businesses in April 1933.

That Streicher's venomous anti-Semitism should win him favor with the Führer was only natural, because both men were prey to similar fantasies— lurid visions of Jewish depravity that were, in fact, mere projections of their own obsessive anxieties and cravings. In *Mein Kampf*, Hitler dwelt pruriently on the supposed lechery of Jews, writing in one passage, "With satanic joy in his face, the black-haired Jewish youth lurks in wait for the unsuspecting girl, whom he defiles with his blood, thus stealing her from her people." Such images reflected Hitler's erotic fantasies just as his feverish descriptions of the political objectives of Jews mirrored his own brutal ambitions. At one point in *Mein Kampf*, he envisioned the result of Jewish world domination in terms that precisely forecast the eventual fate of Poland at the hands of the Nazis. Once Jews had seized control of a state, he insisted, they would seek to "exterminate the national intelligentsia and, by robbing the peoples of their natural intellectual leadership, make them ripe for the slave's lot of permanent subjugation."

Streicher, however, outdid even the Führer at projecting his own vicious tendencies onto the Jews. He never tired of maligning them as greedy and lascivious, yet he was a flagrant example of both qualities. To enrich himself and expand his publishing empire—he eventually acquired ten newspapers in addition to *Der Stürmer*—he took part in a larcenous scheme to intimidate Jews into surrendering their homes and businesses at no more than one-tenth of their value. In less than a month in 1938, Streicher and his cohorts bought and sold 569 pieces of property, including a synagogue, pocketing some 21 million marks (or around $8.4 million, given an exchange rate for the mark of about forty cents). Streicher alone bought an entire factory for one-twentieth its face value. Among the other fruits of his labor was a country estate near Lake Constance so luxurious, it was said, that its pigsty alone was worth more than a single-family house.

Meanwhile, Streicher was earning a reputation as a sadist and a voluptuary. He touted himself as a man of refinement who wrote poetry, dabbled in watercolors, loved animals, and rarely drank. Yet he sometimes walked to his office in bathing trunks and was seldom seen striding through his gau without a riding whip of rhinoceros hide, which he brandished to cow subordinates and punish enemies. On one occasion, he burst into the Nuremberg jail and severely beat a political opponent in his cell. "Now I am relieved," he said afterward. "I really needed that." Such behavior seemed closely linked to his obsession with sex and his own potency. He not only kept a string of mistresses and propositioned any woman who took his fancy, but amassed a large collection of pornography and conducted lurid interviews. He went to the concentration camp at Dachau to question inmates about their sexual fantasies and visited jails to cross-examine juvenile delinquents about masturbation.

Through it all, Hitler stood by Streicher, praising him as a "friend and comrade in arms." As early as 1925, in answer to objections about Streicher and other crude Old Fighters, the Führer had written, "I do not consider it to be the task of a political leader to attempt to improve upon, or even to fuse together, the human material lying ready to his hand." In fact, he preferred working with defective material. Subordinates who had "flaws in the weave," as he put it, were more likely to be grateful for his patronage and mindful of his authority.

Hitler's Dream City

Hitler dreamed of a capital city of monuments and public buildings grander than any in the world. He called it Germania, and, once in power, he gave Albert Speer the daunting task of renovating Berlin to fulfill his architectural fantasies. The Führer used Paris, Vienna, and Rome as models but insisted that Germania surpass those cities in size and splendor. "I do this to restore to each individual German his self-respect," he explained. "We are not inferior; we are the complete equals of every other nation."

The massiveness of the planned structures, however, diminished the human qualities that other architects of the era were beginning to emphasize. Hitler seemed blind to the need for scale, green spaces, residential areas, and smoothly flowing traffic—all desirable features of urban life. Even after the outbreak of war, he insisted that work on Germania continue. Models were created *(right)*, but the rival demands of wartime production made construction impossible.

A 1939 photograph shows Germania as it was envisioned by Hitler and modeled by Speer. Running through the heart of the city, a boulevard 400 feet wide and three miles long links a triumphal arch *(above)* and a mountainous domed hall *(center)*.

On handing Speer sketches of an arch *(above)* and an assembly hall *(right)* in 1936, Hitler explained: "I made these ten years ago. I saved them because I never doubted that some day I would build these two edifices." The arch, inspired by the 160-foot-high Arc de Triomphe in the city of Paris, was to rise 400 feet, and the names of 1.8 million Germans killed in the Great War were to be chiseled into its granite. The domed hall would have held Saint Peter's in Rome several times over.

In the model at left, a tree-lined plaza extending east and west through the city ends at the Brandenburg Gate *(center)*. In the background is a massive chancellery, intended to replace the one Speer had finished in 1939.

At right, eleven government ministries flank the avenue between the assembly hall, called the Great Dome *(above)*, and the memorial arch. The large structure in the foreground is a railroad station. Visitors stepping from it, wrote Speer, would be "stunned by the urban scene and thus the power of the Reich."

After arranging Hitler's flower-strewn entrance to Nuremberg for a 1927 rally *(above)*, bald Julius Streicher stands little noticed behind the Führer's car. A dedicated early Nazi, Streicher edited the anti-Semitic weekly *Der Stürmer*. The front page at left carries the slogan, "The Jews are our misfortune!"

Streicher's dissolute behavior was rivaled by that of another flamboyant aide to Hitler, Robert Ley, a chemist by training who had joined the party in Cologne in 1924, at the age of thirty-four, and had become gauleiter for the Rhineland district. A stutterer who could nonetheless stir a crowd, Ley was short of stature and florid of face, reflecting his hard drinking and frequent emotional outbursts—traits that may have been exacerbated by a head wound he received during the world war when his plane was shot down. As a gauleiter, he cultivated a fierce reputation by mercilessly baiting Jews in his district; one associate called him the "bulldog of the party." Under Hitler's approving eye, he steadily expanded his turf. In 1932, he claimed the top organizational post in the party. And when the Nazis came to power the following year, he sought to broaden his base by seizing control of the Prussian state council. He was thwarted in that bid by Göring, who claimed Prussia as his personal domain, but Ley soon located a more profitable outlet for his ambitions: He emerged as head of the German Labor Front, the party apparatus that replaced the traditional trade unions and, at its peak, controlled more than 25 million workers and employers, constituting the largest mass organization in the Reich.

By dipping into the Labor Front's bulging treasury of membership dues—which by 1939 exceeded 500 million marks—Ley launched a host of commercial ventures in the organization's name. The Labor Front sold insurance through ten different companies, published newspapers and books, constructed houses, operated one of the first modern supermarkets, and built a factory to manufacture Hitler's vaunted *Volkswagen*, or people's car. Such far-ranging enterprises, combined with Ley's efforts to "feed the souls" of German workers through cultural activities sponsored by the Labor Front subsidiary known as Strength through Joy, earned him a reputation as a social visionary. Hitler once called him "my greatest idealist." All the while, Ley was skimming a fortune from the Labor Front's coffers. Although he liked to refer to himself as a "poor working man," he lived like a tycoon in several lavish villas filled with the most expensive furniture and traveled from place to place in his own rail car.

Financial indiscretions aside, Ley's private conduct was hardly a credit to the regime. He consumed alcohol so freely that detractors referred to him as the *Reichstrunkenbold*, or Reich Lush. When the Duke and Duchess of Windsor arrived from England in 1937 to tour Germany as guests of the Labor Front, an inebriated Ley chauffeured them around the workers' barracks at a plant outside Munich. "He drove the car through the locked gates," recalled an aide, "and then raced up and down at full speed between the barracks, scaring the hell out of the workers and nearly running over several. The next day, Hitler told Göring to take over the

Windsors' visit before Ley killed them." With no evident sense of irony, Ley launched a Labor Front campaign in 1939 to discourage drinking. "Moderation is not enough," he proclaimed. "We must be radical in abstinence." His behavior at home, meanwhile, was immoderate in the extreme. In 1938, he had cast off his first wife in favor of a younger, more alluring successor named Inge. He took such pride in her tall blond elegance that he would entertain visitors at their residence near Berlin by drawing back curtains to reveal a life-size oil painting of her in the nude. Reportedly, he once tried to show her off in the flesh by ripping the clothes from her back.

For the most part, Hitler ignored such scandalous behavior by his aides or dismissed their transgressions lightly. (He disapproved of Ley's drinking and smoking but let him off with scoldings.) On rare occasions, however, when the reputation of one of his top lieutenants was at stake, Hitler intervened decisively. In the early days of the regime, Hermann Göring appeared frequently in the company of a German actress named Emmy Sonnemann, who was separated from her husband. She eventually obtained a divorce, but Göring seemed in no hurry to marry her, haunted as he was by the memory of his first wife, Karin, who had died of tuberculosis in 1931. Such was Göring's grief that he established a sumptuous estate in his wife's honor north of Berlin. Known as Karinhall, it cost the government some 15 million marks and included a granite mausoleum for her remains. The forbearing Emmy sometimes joined Göring there. Hitler could sympathize with Göring's dilemma—he himself was consorting with one woman, Eva Braun, while worshiping the memory of another, his niece Geli Raubal, who had committed suicide in 1931. But the Führer decided that Göring, as his most conspicuous paladin, would have to present an impeccable domestic front. Early in 1935, he made it clear that it was time for Göring and Sonnemann to exchange vows. That April, they were married, although Göring confessed sheepishly to one of the guests that he was taking the leap only "at the behest of the Führer."

Three years later, Hitler again interfered in the personal affairs of a top aide, this time to save the marriage of Joseph and Magda Goebbels. Magda was one of Hitler's favorite hostesses, and the six Goebbels children called Hitler "Uncle Führer." He extolled the couple as a model for the nation, conveniently overlooking Joseph's frequent and notorious dalliances with movie actresses and Magda's own occasional and more discreet affairs. By October of 1938, the propaganda minister had fallen so deeply in love with his latest mistress, the Czech actress Lida Baarova, that he was ready to give up his post and go abroad with her. Magda learned of the depth of his passion from one of her own admirers—her husband's young deputy, Karl Hanke, who handed her a dossier he had compiled on his boss's indis-

Decorations helped to define the pecking order in the Nazi hierarchy. The Golden Party Badge with Oak Leaves *(top)* was worn by Adolf Hitler's long-time supporters and was also awarded to some notable latecomers, including Albert Speer. The Blood Order Medal *(center)* was reserved for Old Fighters such as Himmler, Hess, and Göring who had taken part in the 1923 Munich putsch. The Golden Hitler Youth Badge of Honor with Oak Leaves *(bottom)* went to administrators such as Robert Ley who contributed to the nazification of Germany after Hitler had come to power.

cretions, including copies of love letters. To avoid a sensational scandal that might expose the hypocrisy of the regime's professed commitment to traditional family values, Hitler put his foot down, insisting that Goebbels break with Baarova and remain with his wife and children. Meanwhile, the third member of Hitler's trusted triumvirate, Heinrich Himmler, had become permanently estranged from his wife, Margarete. As it turned out, Himmler never sought a divorce. Instead, he carried on a long-term affair with his secretary that eventually yielded two illegitimate children.

One of the few close aides to Hitler who kept up an appearance of bourgeois domesticity was Deputy Führer Rudolf Hess, who lived modestly with his first and only wife in suburban Munich. Yet this cozy hearth earned Hess little credit with his boss, who derided the tastelessness of its

The leader of the German Labor Front, Robert Ley (*second from left*), **inspects a common washbasin at one of the vacation lodges run by his organization. Ley vowed to "extend the rights of the worker," but Labor Front members were forbidden to strike and had to pay hefty dues.**

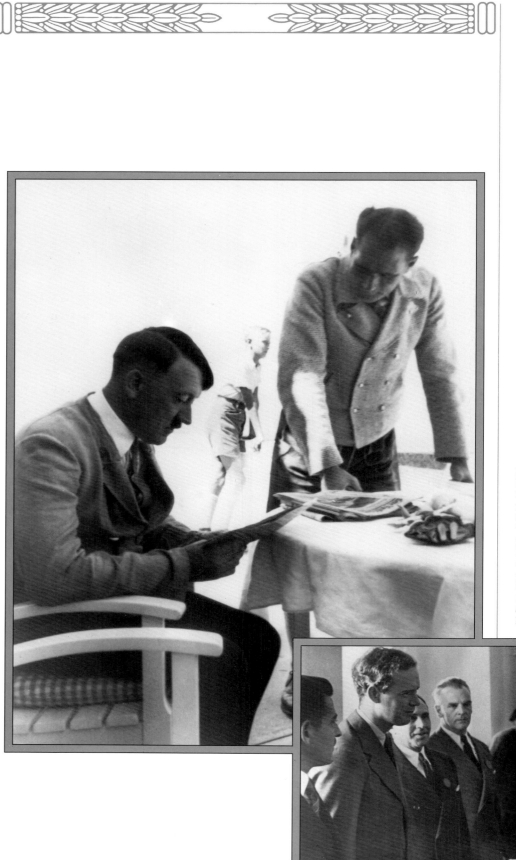

Rudolf Hess lingers expectantly by the breakfast table at the Berghof as Hitler reads the morning papers. Convinced that it was his solemn duty to "surrender to the Führer" and passively carry out his orders, Hess exercised little initiative as deputy führer. He played a prominent role only at ceremonial functions such as the 1935 reception for a fellow aviator, the American Charles Lindbergh (*facing Hess below*).

simple furnishings. The place so offended the aesthetic sensibilities of the Führer, according to one insider, that in 1934 Hitler declared that Hess could not be designated his successor because his house "betrayed such a lack of feeling for art and culture." In truth, Hess seemed an unlikely candidate to succeed Hitler from the start. Like most of the others in Hitler's inner circle, Hess was an Old Fighter—his forehead still bore the scar of a beer mug aimed at Hitler but faithfully intercepted by Hess during a tumultuous rally in 1921. Hess, however, lacked the combative intensity of such fellow fighters as Streicher and Ley. Only his eyes, burning from deep-set sockets under bushy dark eyebrows, betrayed his fanaticism.

At heart, Hess was a follower rather than a leader. He had been searching for a hero to worship since his student days at the University of Munich. When he met Hitler in 1920, at the age of twenty-six, he knew at once that he had found his champion. He felt a delirious delight, he said later, "as though overcome by a vision." His wife recalled that after hearing Hitler speak, Hess returned to their boardinghouse shouting ecstatically, "The man, the man!" Hess became the sixteenth member of the Nazi party and was slavish in his devotion to Hitler. "Everybody knows that Hitler is always right," he said later, "and that he will always be right." After Hitler's unsuccessful coup attempt in 1923—the so-called Beer Hall Putsch—Hess joined his master in prison, where he set down a large portion of Hitler's rambling testimonial, *Mein Kampf.* Hess acted thereafter as Hitler's personal secretary, addressing him by the familiar *du* and serving selflessly as his confidant and alter ego. By one account, it was Hess who originated the honorific *Führer*, or leader.

After Hitler took office in 1933, Hess was happy to remain in his shadow, albeit with formal titles. In addition to appointing him deputy chief of the party, the Führer named Hess to his cabinet as Reich minister without portfolio. Hess shuffled stacks of paper and put into formal language and signed many of the decrees handed down by the Führer, but he seldom attempted to shape those decrees or assert real power. This timidity may explain his appeal to Hitler, who feared the emergence of a compelling rival. Hess's greatest moments came at mass meetings, when, with arm outstretched in salute and eyes aglow, he introduced his Führer.

Increasingly, during the late 1930s, Hess supplemented his faith in the Führer by turning to the pseudosciences that flourished under nazism. He consulted homeopathic doctors, asked a fortuneteller to chart his future by the stars, and suspended a magnet over his bed to draw off harmful auras and restore his sexual vigor. Hess was so fussy about what he ate that, when he dined with Hitler, he brought his own specially prepared "bio-dynamic" meal—until the Führer, himself a food faddist, discovered this impertinence and forbade it. Hess shared another foible with the Führer—a tendency to dwell obsessively on his pet topics. Hitler soon wearied of Hess's occult talk. "With Hess," he observed, "every conversation becomes an unbearably tormenting strain."

The deputy führer's growing preoccupation with folk medicine and other mystic matters created fresh opportunities for his alert and ambitious aide, Martin Bormann. A short, squat man with hunched shoulders, thinning dark hair, and an unassuming manner, Bormann was the least known of the leading Nazis. Because of his drab appearance and rasping voice, he proved utterly ineffective as a public speaker and wisely shunned the limelight. The government-controlled press rarely mentioned his name and, when it did, sometimes misspelled it. Yet by assiduously attending to a host of financial and bureaucratic details that Hess and Hitler gladly delegated, Bormann made himself indispensable and quietly emerged as the Führer's right-hand man.

Bormann began his dogged ascent soon after joining the party in 1927, when he was twenty-six years old. A high-school dropout, he had joined a right-wing vigilante group after the war and served a year in prison for assisting in the political assassination of his former elementary-school teacher. As a Nazi functionary, Bormann soon got a hand on the party purse strings and set up a relief fund to aid comrades injured in the bloody brawls that marked Hitler's rise to power. In 1929, Bormann further advanced his cause by marrying Gerda Buch. Her father chaired the Nazi tribunal responsible for maintaining party discipline and stood close enough to the Führer to warrant Hitler's presence at the wedding.

Admitted to the inner circle himself in 1933 as Hess's deputy, Bormann adroitly seized an important lever of power by taking charge of Hitler's personal finances. He tapped a new source of income by arranging to have a royalty paid to Hitler for each postage stamp on which the Führer's likeness appeared. The royalty was only a fraction of a pfennig per stamp but eventually amounted to millions of marks.

A far more lucrative payoff came from a special slush fund administered by Bormann. Known as the Hitler *Spende*, it consisted of contributions solicited from industrialists who were profiting enormously from German rearmament. During the first year alone, more than 100 million marks poured into the coffers. Bormann prudently avoided dipping into the fund for his own enrichment; instead, he used the money to curry favor with party notables and, above all, with the Führer. It was Bormann who doled out cash for the transformation of Hitler's modest retreat at Berchtesgaden into an opulent estate. By Speer's estimate, one part of this project alone—the access road and elevator shaft that led from the Berghof to Hitler's isolated clifftop teahouse—cost between 20 million and 30 million marks. Skeptics in Hitler's circle gibed that Bormann had started a gold rush in reverse on the mountain. "He doesn't find any," they said, "he spends it."

Lavish expenditure was not the only way in which Bormann sought to endear himself to Hitler. He knew that the Führer detested paperwork, so he carried a notebook and pencil at all times to jot down Hitler's orders, questions, and passing remarks. Even at the lunch table, observed a colleague, Bormann kept his notepad on his lap, "all ears and all scribbling."

Martin Bormann *(right)* gets in a word with Hitler as the German delegation arrives at the Munich Conference in 1938. Known as the Brown Eminence for his political cunning and the color of his party uniform, Bormann was so jealous of his access to Hitler that he never took a vacation except with the Führer.

No question or request was too trivial for a Bormann follow-up. If the Führer casually wondered about the ingredients of a sauce, for example, his assistant provided him with the recipe.

Quietly, Bormann increased his authority by functioning not merely as Hitler's scribe but as his editor. He translated the Führer's rambling spoken directives into coherent orders and saw that they were carried out immediately. For future reference, he transferred Hitler's comments to a card file classified by cue phrases. When issuing subsequent orders, Bormann could consult this file and choose what suited him from the Führer's often-contradictory statements. At the same time, he won Hitler's gratitude—and subtly influenced his decisions—by offering the Führer concise summaries of matters requiring his action. "Bormann's proposals are so precisely worked out that I have only to say yes or no," remarked the Führer. "With him I deal in ten minutes with a pile of documents for which with another man I should need hours."

Bormann spared no effort to ingratiate himself with Hitler. At the Berghof, he would even share the Führer's vegetarian meals, then retire to his own nearby chalet to feast furtively on Wiener schnitzel or porkchops. Speer observed that Bormann outdid all the other sycophants in Hitler's entourage—and compensated for it by treating his own subordinates as if they were "cows or oxen." Among those he tyrannized was his wife, Gerda, whom he addressed cloyingly in letters as "Mummy Girl" but regularly humiliated in front of friends and strangers. He mortified guests at the

Berghof by whistling through his fingers whenever he wanted her. Nonetheless, she was such a staunch Nazi helpmate that she bore him ten children—the first one named Adolf after his godfather—and encouraged her husband to augment the racial stock further by impregnating the movie-actress mistress he took during the war *(pages 118-119)*.

The ascent of Bormann from obscurity to prominence in the Nazi hierarchy typified the vicious maneuvering that Hitler and his aides glorified as an evolutionary process, ensuring the survival of the fittest. As Bormann once remarked, "It is not honesty that in real life overcomes dishonesty. In the harsh struggle for existence, the stronger, the harder capacity for self-assertion daily gains the victory." Hitler resorted to similar language to rationalize the crude and chaotic rivalries among his subordinates—contests that diverted energies that might otherwise have been directed toward important matters of policy. "I imagine myself to be a gardener," Hitler once said, "who looks over his fence at the garden and watches as the plants themselves struggle for the light." Hitler's press secretary, Otto Dietrich, recalled that the Führer liked to portray his lieutenants as men who had "risen by natural selection out of the political struggle." As the dominant members of this select breed continued to vie for supremacy, the argument went, Germany's government would "advance to the highest possible point of evolution."

Such was the theory. Yet the reality was something else. As Dietrich lamented, "Hitler created in the political leadership of Germany the greatest confusion that has ever existed in a civilized state." In fact, Hitler had little interest in resolving the confusion—and did much to compound it. Intent on maintaining supremacy, he kept his subordinates at loggerheads, making sure that no one champion emerged to knock him from his perch.

Hitler's tendency to encourage discord among his disciples, combined with his basic contempt for bureaucratic matters, transformed Germany's once-orderly administrative fabric into a crazy quilt of conflicting appointments and overlapping jurisdictions. Hitler balanced every government office with a Nazi party post of comparable status, established bewildering new authorities with grandiose titles, issued vague or contradictory instructions to all concerned, and then watched with some glee as his underlings grappled with the consequences.

In the area of propaganda, for example, Goebbels had to put up with interference from Alfred Rosenberg, the party ideologue, who among other distinctions held the impressive-sounding titles of director of the Reich Office for the Promotion of German Literature, and Führer's delegate for the general intellectual and philosophical education and instruction of the

The party ideologue, Alfred Rosenberg, welcomes foreign correspondents to a banquet in 1938. Prickly and pedantic, Rosenberg feuded endlessly with rivals in the party, and Hitler only tolerated him. "He valued me very much," Rosenberg said, "but he did not like me."

National Socialist party. Neither job amounted to much. The Reich office was one of twenty-one different offices in the party and government involved in the censorship of books, and the education post was little more than a fancy label pinned on by Hitler, who admired Rosenberg's success as an author of racist tracts even though he found his prose impenetrable. Tall, dark, and dourly intellectual, the Estonian-born Rosenberg seemed an unlikely candidate to champion the theory of Nordic supremacy. Yet his 1930 book devoted to that concept, *The Myth of the Twentieth Century*, eventually sold more than a million copies and ranked second only to *Mein Kampf* as a Nazi gospel. In Rosenberg's presence, Hitler praised it as a "very intelligent book," but he privately professed wonderment at its popularity. (Ironically, a number of Hitler's associates were similarly baffled by the appeal of *Mein Kampf*.) Whatever his reservations about the author, Hitler protected the politically inept Rosenberg from his many influential detractors, one of whom labeled him a "stuck-up crackpot ninny."

Rosenberg was a mild irritant within the regime compared with Hitler's caustic protégé, Joachim von Ribbentrop. A former wine merchant, Ribbentrop acquired the aristocratic *von* in his name in 1925, when he was thirty-two years old. He persuaded an aunt to adopt him after her husband had been knighted. Seven years later, he joined forces with Hitler, who was impressed both by Ribbentrop's social connections and by his presumed

Foreign Minister Joachim von Ribbentrop *(center)* shares the Führer's glee after signing a nonaggression pact with the Soviet Union in August 1939. Ribbentrop boasted that he could "fill a chest" with the treaties he had violated. The Russian treaty lasted twenty-two months.

mastery of foreign affairs—Ribbentrop had written a political newsletter for business contacts abroad, spoke English and French, and had traveled as far as Canada. His expertise was largely illusory, but, as one of Hitler's associates remarked, the Führer then regarded anyone who had just returned from a holiday in Italy as a "foreign-affairs expert." Hitler gave Ribbentrop a succession of increasingly important assignments: chief adviser on foreign affairs in 1933, ambassador at large in 1935, and ambassador to England in 1936. All this undermined the position of the Reich's official foreign minister, Constantin von Neurath, a conservative diplomat who feared the consequences of Hitler's aggressive international agenda. In February 1938, a few weeks before annexing Austria, Hitler elevated Ribbentrop to the top spot in Neurath's stead.

The promotion was guaranteed to antagonize foreign diplomats as well as the Führer's domestic aides. Ribbentrop was incorrigibly arrogant and self-absorbed; like Hitler, his idea of a diplomatic conversation was little more than a monologue. "One could not talk to Ribbentrop," wrote the French ambassador, André François-Poncet. "He only listened to himself." Ribbentrop's Nazi colleagues were even less complimentary. Fed up with his aristocratic airs, they called him "von Ribbensnob." His only defender of note was Hitler, and he needed no other. He had the courtier's knack of listening carefully to Hitler's pronouncements, memorizing the essential points, and later playing them back as if they were his own, thus pleasing the Führer, who loved to hear his opinions echoed. Diplomatic gaffes, such as greeting the king of England with "Heil Hitler!" only endeared him to the Führer. Hitler squelched critical remarks from the other paladins, all of whom loathed Ribbentrop, by asserting that Ribbentrop ranked above Otto von Bismarck, the revered nineteenth-century German statesman. Still, the Führer himself was not above poking private fun at Ribbentrop. "If Hitler was displeased with him," one of the foreign minister's aides recalled, "Ribbentrop went sick or took to his bed like a hysterical woman."

As foreign minister, Ribbentrop used his influence with Hitler to wrest from Goebbels responsibility for the conduct of all propaganda abroad. Goebbels was incensed. When movers from the Foreign Ministry showed up at the Propaganda Ministry to claim the relevant records, they found the offices barricaded. Forced to intervene in the dispute, Hitler summoned his warring aides and ordered them to sit down together and work it out. Three hours later, they emerged without agreement. Hitler then dictated a compromise and added a ukase that forbade "once and for all the bringing of differences of opinion to my person." After a brief respite, the tug of war between Goebbels and Ribbentrop resumed.

Meanwhile, Göring, too, was coping with challenges to his authority. In

1936, he had emerged as the czar of the German economy when Hitler named him director of the Four-Year Plan, an ambitious attempt to prepare the nation for war by making it economically self-sufficient by 1940. The appointment did not silence Göring's opponents, however. Among his persistent critics was the Reich minister of economics, Hjalmar Schacht, who looked askance at Göring's spendthrift ways. (Expenditures on the Luftwaffe, in particular, skyrocketed as Göring's power increased.) In late 1937, Schacht conceded defeat in his feud with Göring and resigned his post. His successor was the amenable Walther Funk, a one-time editor and assistant to Goebbels at the Propaganda Ministry. Schacht derided Funk as a feckless "homosexual and alcoholic," and, indeed, Funk drank too much and was given to indiscreet homosexual affairs. But he was a loyal functionary who lionized Hitler, deferred to Göring, and endeared himself to others in the hierarchy by enthusiastically supporting anti-Semitic measures despite his once-cordial relations with Jews in the business world.

After Schacht stepped down, sniping continued between Göring and

Engineer Fritz Todt *(center)* **shows Hitler the model of a bridge on the autobahn, one of several construction projects masterminded by Todt before his death in an air crash in 1942. "He was," said an associate, "a man you could rely on."**

Robert Ley, who was infringing on Göring's claim to economic supremacy through his assorted Labor Front ventures. As war approached, Göring argued that some of the Labor Front money being used to better workers' lives through such programs as Strength through Joy ought to go into building weapons. "The Labor Front should make more strength," Göring insisted, "and less joy." To complicate matters for Göring, the fortunes of his Four-Year Plan depended to a large extent on a man who was nominally his subordinate but who in fact reported directly to Hitler—the technocrat Fritz Todt. A first-rate engineer, Todt had won Hitler's admiration in the mid-1930s by supervising the construction of 2,000 miles of autobahns, superhighways designed to expedite military as well as civilian traffic. Although Todt subsequently wielded immense power as an architect of the Four-Year Plan and the director of vast military construction projects—including the Siegfried Line guarding Germany's western border—he lived quietly and avoided intrigue. Almost alone among Hitler's aides, he "withstood the temptation to sycophancy," observed Speer. Even so, Hitler paid Todt a "respect bordering on reverence."

Mindful of Todt's talents and of his high standing with Hitler, Göring reached an accommodation with the engineer, who pledged not to subvert Göring's authority as chief of the Four-Year Plan. But Göring was in no mood for compromise when Streicher challenged him on a personal level. After Göring's daughter, Edda, was born in 1937, Streicher published a charge that Göring was impotent and that Edda had been conceived by artificial insemination. This calumny touched a live nerve in Göring, who had been shot in the groin during the Beer Hall Putsch in 1923. The injury left him addicted to morphine for a time and made him fear impotence.

The insult to Göring proved to be a major tactical blunder by Streicher, whose stock in the party was at an all-time low. Hess and Bormann wanted to get rid of him because he refused to obey dictates from party headquarters. Other Nazi potentates lived in fear that Streicher might denounce them in his newspaper for insufficient anti-Semitic zeal. Himmler even had his Gestapo keep Streicher under surveillance, documenting every potential misstep. Armed with such material, Göring took dead aim at Streicher and appointed a special party commission to examine the corrupt gauleiter's business transactions and personal behavior. The commission went to Nuremberg for hearings in 1940 equipped with wiretap records and other incriminating documents provided by the Gestapo. Following its inquiry, the commission found Streicher "unfit for leadership." Because he had failed to cut the national party in on profits from the confiscation of Jewish properties, he was judged guilty, among other transgressions, of excess greed. With Hitler's reluctant approval, Streicher was suspended

from his post as gauleiter and banished from Nuremberg for five years. He remained editor of *Der Stürmer* and spewed his anti-Semitic vitriol at long distance from the comfort of his country estate.

Göring's success in calling Streicher to account confirmed what had long been apparent to Nazi insiders—that after Hitler, Göring was the man to be reckoned with in the Reich, both in terms of party leverage and national prestige. For some time, Göring had been Hitler's presumed heir. But as war loomed in the late summer of 1939, the normally secretive Führer felt compelled to announce his plans for succession—if only to discourage enemies at home or abroad who might try to halt the German war effort at one blow by eliminating Hitler. On September 1, 1939, he convened the Reichstag to declare that he had invaded Poland. "If anything should befall me in this struggle," he added, "then my successor shall be party member Göring." Deputy Führer Hess was not forgotten: Should Göring fall, Hitler told the Reichstag, Hess was to take his place. Left unexplained was just how Hess would assert that right when he had already yielded much of his responsibility to the shadowy Bormann. Even Göring's status as successor was less than definitive, for it had no basis in law. The office of Führer was inseparable from the man who had created it, and once Hitler was gone there would be no way to ensure an orderly transfer of power.

Whatever its practical consequences, Hitler's decision to anoint Göring as his heir demonstrated his confidence in Göring's loyalty. Aware of the enormous challenges that lay ahead, the congenitally suspicious and re-clusive Führer felt the need to tighten the knot that bound him to his most powerful lieutenant. "I am not a lonely man," he remarked around this time. "I have the best friend in the world. I have Göring!" In truth, Göring's devotion to Hitler remained that of a lackey pining for rewards and dread-ing punishment. As one correspondent remarked, even after Göring emerged as Hitler's official successor, he never forgot that the Führer had the "power to eliminate him just by the scratch of a pen." Having inculcated such terror and distrust in his closest confidants, Hitler could hardly expect them to advise him frankly and fearlessly in time of conflict.

If anything, Hitler grew more isolated in the years leading up to the war and came to regard the coming struggle as a personal crusade whose risks and rewards were his alone. Long after that crusade reached its fiery conclusion, Albert Speer would recall prophetic words once uttered by the Führer. Sitting in the bay window of his Berchtesgaden retreat and gazing at the stark Alpine landscape in the dying evening light, Hitler had stated, "There are two possibilities for me: to win through with all my plans or to fail. If I win, I shall be one of the greatest men in history. If I fail, I shall be condemned, despised, and damned." ✠

Hermann Göring confronts Julius Streicher at the Nurem-berg rally in 1937, before their hostility erupted into an open feud. When challenged by adver-saries, Göring dropped his genial facade and lived up to his reputation as Hitler's "iron man."

A Fatal Way with Beauties

Throughout his public career, Adolf Hitler's bachelor status sparked lively speculation about his romantic life. Frequently asked why he had never married, the Führer responded that a statesman should hold himself aloof from petty domestic distractions. "My bride," he declared, "is Germany."

Beneath that lofty, politically shrewd posture lurked an emotional snake pit. Hitler's feelings toward women were tortured and wildly contradictory. He loved to surround himself with dazzling females and, according to his press chief, "rather enjoyed being suspected of many amours—although no one in his immediate circle ever noticed signs of such intimacies."

On the contrary, the Führer's aversion to sexual intimacy was so obvious to his associates that many of them privately believed he was homosexual. Aside from courtly hand kisses and avuncular pats on the arm, he assiduously avoided physical contact with women. In 1924, when a woman at a New Year's Eve party maneuvered him under the mistletoe and planted a kiss on his mouth, Hitler's expression of revulsion shocked the revelers into embarrassed silence. "I shall never forget the look of astonishment and horror on Hitler's face," said his chagrined host.

And yet pornography reportedly fascinated the Führer, and he was determined to present himself as a man of overpowering virility. A woman visitor idly browsing through his Obersalzberg library one day was startled when Hitler made a sudden bid for her attention with a stiff Nazi salute and a suggestive tirade. "My arm is like granite, rigid and unbending," he boasted loudly. "I am hard. For two hours I can keep my arm stretched out. I marvel at my own power."

Hitler was convinced that women found such displays irresistible, and he was equally confident that he possessed a unique personal magnetism—a pervasive impression bolstered by a worshipful public that treated him as a sexual cult hero.

The women who got close enough to develop a more informed opinion had differing reactions. Doubtless many shared the assessment of one female acquaintance who sized up the Führer as a "neuter." Others, however, were genuinely attracted to him—some fatally so. Beginning with a seventeen-year-old shopgirl who tried to hang herself in 1927, after a rift with Hitler, at least six women who had become closely involved with him over the years either committed suicide or made serious attempts to do so.

A birthday card signed by Hitler accompanied a bouquet to a woman friend in 1925. The Führer loved to give flowers—and was equally quick with flowery compliments. "How can a man not be in seventh heaven with such a woman!" he rhapsodized over blond Inge Ley (*right*), the wife of labor leader Robert Ley. Deeply unhappy in her marriage, Inge ended her life by jumping from a window.

When Geli Raubal, Hitler's niece, came to live with her uncle in 1929, the grim party leader was briefly transformed into an ardent swain. Often available for a movie, a picnic, or a shopping spree, he mooned about the vivacious girl, said one crony, "like a faithful lamb." This obvious infatuation with someone who was nineteen years his junior set tongues wagging all over the city of Munich. Raubal was widely assumed to be Hitler's mistress, and there were even whispers of perverted sexual practices.

Whatever the precise nature of the relationship, it clearly oppressed Raubal. Hitler's jealousy torpedoed two budding romances and led to furious fights. It was after one such row that she killed herself, at the age of twenty-three. For days, Hitler wildly declared his own intention to commit suicide—and found he could no longer stomach meat. ("It's like eating a corpse," he shuddered.) Eventually, he consoled himself by worshiping Geli Raubal in memory as the "only woman I ever truly loved."

1 As a schoolgirl, Geli Raubal stands between her mother, Angela, who was Hitler's half sister and housekeeper, and her aunt, Paula, his full sister.

2 On a lakeside outing, Raubal flashes a smile at Hitler's official photographer, Heinrich Hoffmann. Much taken with her unspoiled charms, Hoffmann called her an "enchantress."

3 Hitler attends his niece in a rare intimate photograph. When he had to be away, Hitler had her shadowed by party police and spied on by the household staff.

4 Sprawled on the lawn at Hitler's Bavarian hideaway a year or so before her death, an amused Raubal eyes her napping uncle.

5 Raubal shot herself in her bedroom in Hitler's apartment in this building on one of Munich's most exclusive streets. Grief-stricken, the Führer ordered her elegant room sealed as a shrine.

When the horror of Geli Raubal's death faded, Hitler recultivated his taste for female companionship. As star-struck as a schoolboy, he was particularly drawn to actresses and relished the opportunity his prominence gave him to mingle with such luminaries as the tempestuous Renate Mueller and the celebrated Olga Tschechowa.

Newspapers indulged in titillating gossip about these relationships, but Hitler's interest probably arose less from romantic stirrings than from his perception of himself as an artist who belonged in the company of other artists. That attitude extended to other prominent cultural figures, among them architect Gerdy Troost and opera patron Winifred Wagner, the widowed daughter-in-law of his idol, composer Richard Wagner.

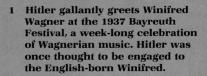

1 Hitler gallantly greets Winifred Wagner at the 1937 Bayreuth Festival, a week-long celebration of Wagnerian music. Hitler was once thought to be engaged to the English-born Winifred.

2 After SS officers had mistreated her Jewish lover, actress Renate Mueller leaped in front of the Führer's car. Her suicide fueled speculation that she had been involved in an affair with Hitler.

3 Flanked by Göring and Goebbels, Hitler attends an art opening with Gerdy Troost, widow of the architect Paul Troost. Entrusted with the interior design of Hitler's residences, she became an influential tastemaker.

4 Olga Tschechowa sits at Hitler's side during a 1939 concert. He often urged friends to leave their wives at home and escort starlets to such functions. "To the greatest warrior belongs the most beautiful woman," he said.

3

4

In the heyday of the Third Reich, few women were as prominently associated with the Führer as Leni Riefenstahl—known to American tabloid readers as "Hitler's Honey." An idolized film star turned director, Riefenstahl was an assertive, multitalented beauty who enjoyed a uniquely privileged relationship with the Führer. Hitler respected her artistry and made sure she was spared the draconian censorship that shackled the rest of the German film industry.

Riefenstahl repaid his faith handsomely with *Triumph of the Will*, a cinematic masterpiece documenting the 1934 party rally at Nuremberg. Widely regarded as the most effective propaganda film of all time, it made Riefenstahl the focus of persistent debate: Was she an artist so dedicated to her work that she was blind to its moral implications or a true believer, eloquently expressing her devotion to the German Reich and its leader?

1   Leni Riefenstahl sets up a shot of Hitler at Nuremberg in 1934. In order to disguise the Führer's dumpy figure, she placed her cameras below him and aimed upward, producing a godlike, larger-than-life image.

2   In 1937, Riefenstahl strolls with Goebbels and Hitler outside of her Berlin home, where she frequently entertained high-ranking Nazi officials.

3   Hitler warmly clasps Riefenstahl's hand in 1936, the year she filmed *Olympia*, an epic documentary of the Berlin Olympics. Controversial because it glorified the Nazi cult of the body, the film took first prize at the 1938 Venice Film Festival—beating Walt Disney's *Snow White*.

4   Riefenstahl, a lifelong fitness devotee, maintained a year-round tan by skiing in swimsuits that showed off a figure toned by ballet and mountaineering.

4

3

In 1932, Hitler's fantasy of an alliance with England was sustained by the addition to his entourage of an intense young British aristocrat with a seemingly prophetic name: Unity Valkyrie Mitford. An avowed fascist, Mitford had a passionate crush on Hitler, who in turn appreciated her strapping Aryan looks and the propaganda value of her patrician background. "This girl is a treasure!" he exclaimed. For seven years, Mitford toured Germany in a car flying the Union Jack and the swastika, cheering lustily at party rallies and submitting anti-Semitic diatribes to Nazi publications. The lark ended on September 3, 1939, when Britain declared war on Germany: She sat on a Munich park bench and shot herself in the head. Mitford survived and lived another nine years, remaining to the end loyal to the Führer.

1 Unity Mitford basks in the company of the scabrously anti-Semitic publisher Julius Streicher, whom even many Nazis considered odious.

2 Photographs of Hitler surround Mitford in her Munich room. "I love him more and more," she gushed in a letter home.

3 Accompanied by her father, Baron Redesdale (*far right*), Mitford is carried off the Channel ferry on her return to England, four months after she attempted suicide.

4 Because her hair hid the wound on her right temple, Mitford's normal appearance led to charges she feigned injury to escape prosecution for "consorting with the king's enemies."

1

2

3

1   Eighteen-year-old Eva Braun flirts for the camera in Heinrich Hoffmann's office in 1930.

2   Photos of Hitler and Braun sit on her neat dressing table. Despite the party's disapproval of cosmetics, she used makeup to enhance what Hoffmann called a "chocolate-box prettiness."

3   Braun took delight in her menagerie of stuffed animals.

4   In a 1938 snapshot, Hitler stands stiffly among Braun's coworkers. She worked for Hoffmann until 1945. Whenever her presence in the Führer's entourage was noticed, she was identified as a representative of the studio.

Removed from the glare of publicity that beamed on Hitler's friendships with glamorous women, his one lasting romance was lost in the shadows. Germans knew almost nothing of the liaison with Eva Braun, a Munich shoolteacher's daughter he had met in 1930, when she was an assistant in Heinrich Hoffmann's photography studio.

To Hitler's intimates, it seemed an unlikely pairing. Slim and girlish, Braun did not match the Führer's taste for voluptuous women. According to Hoffmann, Hitler regard-

ed her as "just another attractive little thing, in whom, in spite of her featherbrained outlook—or perhaps because of it—he found the relaxation and repose he sought."

Braun's feelings were stronger. Determined to marry the man, she set her cap with an intensity that led her to the attributes he prized—unquestioning loyalty and willing submissiveness. Those qualities, combined with a knack for putting the Führer at ease—a formidable feat in itself—enabled her, in time, to prevail over likelier rivals.

4

Eva Braun's campaign to secure Hitler's affections took an emotional toll. In despair over his cavalier treatment of her and his fondness for other women, she twice tried to commit suicide. In 1935, just before the second attempt, she confided bitterly to her diary, "I wish I had never met him."

If Braun's attempts were desperate bids for attention, they worked. Both times, Hitler responded sympathetically. He bought her a house in Munich; and by the end of 1939—a time that coincided with the onset of war and the departure of Unity Mitford, whom she regarded as a serious rival—Braun's position as the Führer's favorite was secure.

But it made for a lonely life. Remaining in the background, she took her place at Hitler's side only in the privacy of his Berghof retreat. Even there, wrote a visitor, she was merely "part of the ambiance, like the canary cage, the rubber tree, and the kitschy wooden clocks."

1 Eva Braun (right) and a pal balance on the side-mounted spare tires of their Mercedes. Left alone for long periods, Braun relied on relatives and women friends for companionship.

2 An avid shutterbug, Braun snaps photographs on an overlook near the Berghof.

3 Braun, third from left between Martin Bormann and press chief Otto Dietrich (in uniform), celebrates New Year's with the group that frequented the Berghof.

4 Hitler's visage glowers from a wall in the quarters he and Braun shared at Berchtesgaden.

5 In a Hoffmann photograph from her album, Braun exercises on the shore of an Alpine lake.

3

4

5

1 Visiting wives, Magda Goebbels (*left*) and Gerda Bormann, join Hitler and Eva Braun for tea in the stone-walled Eagle's Nest.

2 Dressed in a Bavarian folk costume, Braun curtsies to Hitler on the terrace at the Berghof.

3 Hitler stoops to pet Braun's two Scotties. She helped fill time by training her dogs and delighted in showing off their obedience.

4 A picture of domestic tranquillity, Hitler pats the head of little Uschi Schneider, daughter of Braun's best friend. After the war, Hitler promised, "Eva and I will be married and will live in a beautiful house in Linz."

An Erratic Warlord

hortly after the conquest of Poland in 1939, Hitler summoned his senior commanders to the imposing new Reich Chancellery in Berlin and delivered a three-hour harangue, castigating those among them who believed that his aggression would prove unwise. After presenting his strategic reasoning for invading Poland, he turned to a favorite subject—himself. In the coming war against the West, he would be indispensable. "Neither a military man nor a civilian could replace me," Hitler said. "I am convinced of my powers of intellect and decision. No one has ever achieved what I have achieved. I have led the German people to a great height," Hitler intoned, warming to the theme. "I have to choose between victory and destruction. I choose victory. I shall stand or fall in this struggle. I shall shrink from nothing and shall destroy everyone who is opposed to me."

His message was unmistakable. This was to be his war, and he would share it with no one. In particular, he would not share it with the generals, whose pusillanimity he believed was in part responsible for Germany's defeat in 1918. From the first, Hitler let it be known that he would brook no opposition from the military. His commanders would simply do his bidding, without reservation, without hesitancy, and without complaint. "I do not ask my generals to understand my orders," he was to say on another occasion, "but only to carry them out."

Hitler's impatience with the military professionals—coupled with his sense of mission and conviction that he was a military genius—would contribute to the triumphs and disasters that lay ahead for Germany. As the war wore on, he became more engrossed in its daily conduct and increasingly disengaged from his duties as head of state. In response to his growing isolation and the deterioration of the Reich's military fortunes, new men rose in the party hierarchy while established figures fell. By 1943, the time of the Stalingrad crisis, Hitler was waging a war in his head that had less and less to do with the war his armies were fighting in the field.

In a way, Adolf Hitler had been preparing for wartime leadership most of his adult life. As an infantry corporal whose bravery had won him the Iron

Hitler and an aide emerge from a bunker at Felsennest (Rocky Refuge), the Führer's headquarters on the Belgian border during the spring campaign of 1940. When Hitler left Felsennest that June, he proclaimed the bunkers and wooden huts a national monument and had them preserved just as he left them.

Cross First Class in World War I, he had experienced combat and knew the psychology of the common soldier. Both before and after that baptismal experience, he read widely in military history and in the works of outstanding German commanders. Gifted with an extraordinary memory, he held a prodigious amount of technical detail at his disposal. "On matters of army equipment, his knowledge was far superior to that of his military staff," recalled the architect Albert Speer. He not only steeped himself in information about new weapons and vehicles but frequently made valuable suggestions for their improvement. His lack of formal command training was actually an asset, Hitler claimed, for it freed his mind of the stereotypes that shackled the high command. When it came to warfare, he liked to say, "the impossible is always successful; the most unlikely thing is the surest."

In February 1938, he began reorganizing the command structure of the Wehrmacht in preparation for the coming war. He knew that most senior officers strongly opposed his precipitate march toward a conflict they were convinced Germany could not win. Accordingly, he removed the commander in chief of the armed forces, Field Marshal Werner von Blomberg, using Blomberg's marriage to a former prostitute as a pretext. Blomberg's post was abolished, and the War Ministry he had headed was disbanded. Next, Hitler dismissed General Werner von Fritsch, commander in chief of the army, on a trumped-up charge of homosexuality. To succeed Fritsch, he appointed the far more compliant General Walther von Brauchitsch.

Henceforth, Hitler proclaimed, he would "exercise immediate command over the whole armed forces" as Führer and supreme commander. Taking over Blomberg's staff in the War Ministry, he created the High Command of the Armed Forces (OKW). Although army leaders deluded themselves into believing the OKW was an independent military authority with genuine powers of command, it became, in fact, Hitler's personal military staff, charged with seeing that his orders were carried out. How little independent authority it possessed was apparent from the man Hitler selected to head it. He was General Wilhelm Keitel, a sycophantic career officer whose habit of warmly assenting to everything his superiors said to him had earned him the nickname the Nodding Ass. Doubtful of his own command abilities—"I am no field marshal," he once acknowledged ruefully—he soon let himself be reduced to little more than an errand boy.

The other officer whom Hitler would see on an almost daily basis was the chief of the OKW Operations Staff, Brigadier General Alfred Jodl. Far abler than Keitel, General Jodl was also more realistic about the war and less inclined to agree automatically with Hitler's every move. But he, too, was convinced of the Führer's genius and just as determined to suppress dissent in the officer corps. Throughout the war, chiefs of the army high command and field commanders enjoyed a few moments of glory serving Hitler and then fell from grace, but Keitel and Jodl remained at his side, conferring with him daily, transforming his orders into directives, screening him from military realities he did not wish to acknowledge.

The consequences of Hitler's assumption of supreme command became apparent in March 1938, when he ordered the occupation of Austria. The generals objected, fearing that the action would trigger western intervention and war. Hitler ignored them and took charge of the operation. After incorporating Austria, he turned his attention in May to Czechoslovakia. He summoned army leaders to his headquarters and told them bluntly of his intention to invade that country, ostensibly to rescue the German minorities there. Again, the generals were appalled but powerless: The OKW staff had drawn up the plans for invasion without consulting the army. When Lieut. General Ludwig Beck, chief of the army high command, resigned in protest, no one followed his lead. Beck was replaced by the strong-minded and dedicated Lieut. General Franz Halder, whose high professional reputation Hitler hoped would quiet the army unrest.

On the eve of war, therefore, Hitler had a command structure that allowed him to bypass normal channels to turn his wishes into direct action. Yet he did not interfere much in the first phase of the war, the conquest of Poland in September 1939. When he addressed his senior officers ten days before the campaign began, it was largely to assure them that the invasion was inevitable—given the unsatisfied German claims to Danzig and the Polish Corridor—and to stress his conviction that the western powers would not intervene. The Führer impressed Jodl's deputy, General Walter Warlimont. When the commanders presented their operational plans, Warlimont wrote, "Hitler showed himself extremely well informed on all details and did not hesitate to produce further suggestions of his own." But the suggestions remained suggestions, and Hitler limited himself to planning, in detail, the assault on a single bridge at Dirschau.

Even after he had boarded his train, the Führer Special, and headed toward the front, he rarely gave orders or interceded in the conduct of operations. In part, he refrained because the invasion was such a textbook operation; gigantic double pincers trapped most of the Polish forces before they could retreat across the Vistula River. For this campaign, Hitler sensed that he should not meddle with success: He was content to tour the front in visible confirmation of the role he had publicly assumed, as "just the first soldier of the German Reich."

The stunning thirty-six-day Polish campaign boosted the generals' self-confidence. True, Hitler had misjudged Britain and France, which declared war on September 3, but he convinced both himself and his commanders

that the Allies' response was only a token gesture of solidarity with Poland. They had, after all, sat passively behind the Maginot Line during the Polish campaign; surely, they would now agree to a negotiated peace.

When that goal eluded Hitler, he called his commanders together and told them of his plan to launch an autumn offensive in the west. All present, Warlimont noted, "including even Göring, were clearly taken aback." Even if a peace could not be patched together diplomatically, the military leaders had hoped that there would at least be a stalemate in the west until they could build up the forces they believed necessary for a large-scale attack. Hitler announced in a memorandum that the offensive would begin before Christmas. Using considerable strategic imagination, he sketched a plan of attack that stressed mobility and speed. The decisive thrust would be "on the northern flank of the western front, through Luxembourg, Belgium, and Holland," and the key to success would be the armored divisions. They must not let themselves be tied down "among the endless rows of houses in Belgian towns." In fact, they should not attack towns at all but concentrate on maintaining "the flow of the army's advance, to prevent fronts from becoming stable." So long as they did not let the fighting degenerate into a war of positions, there was no reason why German armies could not continue operations well into the winter.

The generals were alarmed. They thought Hitler vastly overestimated German preparedness and grossly underestimated the forces that France and Britain could put in the field. Brauchitsch sought an audience with Hitler and argued against an autumn offensive: Munitions and artillery were in dangerously short supply; only five armored divisions were fully prepared; a mechanized attack of the kind Hitler envisioned would surely bog down in the autumn rains. None of the arguments had any effect on

Hitler (*left*) sets the pace for an escort of army brass at maneuvers in Austria during the spring of 1939. When Czechoslovakia capitulated without a fight, Hitler exulted, "I shall go down in history as the greatest German."

Hitler. "It rains on the enemy, too," he remarked. When Brauchitsch, trying to salvage something from the meeting, said that the high command would be grateful for an understanding that it alone would be in charge of running the campaign, Hitler maintained an icy silence.

As it happened, bad weather—combined with foot-dragging by the army command—forced postponement of the invasion of the West until January, and then until spring. Hitler's first opportunity to exercise independent command came in April of 1940, when he invaded Denmark and Norway. His interest in a Scandinavian incursion had been kindled the previous November, when the Russians attacked Finland. He feared that British forces might use the pretext of aiding the Finns to occupy Norway—thus outflanking Germany from the north, bottling up the Reich's Baltic Fleet, and threatening the vital flow of iron ore from Sweden. Hitler ordered the preparation of Weser Exercise, as it was code-named, specifying that operations in the north would be "under my immediate and personal influence." He meant that so literally—and excluded the dubious high com-

During the last days of peace, in August 1939, Hitler receives a firsthand briefing on the West Wall, Germany's unfinished line of defense against an attack from France. At his immediate right is engineer Fritz Todt, who oversaw construction of the wall.

Below, Hitler confers with Foreign Minister Joachim von Ribbentrop outside the Führer Special, Hitler's rolling headquarters for the advance across Poland. The train boasted a handsomely appointed banquet car, shown at top right, in which Hitler entertained heads of state, as well as open cars equipped with antiaircraft guns. At bottom right, the supreme commander takes his morning constitutional accompanied by an aide.

mand so effectively—that Halder complained in his diary, "Not a single word has passed between the Führer and the commander in chief of the army on this subject!"

When the invasion was launched on April 9, Denmark fell easily, but the Norwegian campaign started poorly. Newly arrived British naval and land forces sank ten German destroyers and cut off the German 3d Mountain Division in the Norwegian port of Narvik. General Warlimont recalled that the crisis revealed "all Hitler's deficiencies of character and military knowledge." The Führer panicked. He fired off frantic and contradictory directives to his headquarters staff to be relayed to General Eduard Dietl, commander of the land forces at Narvik. One order told Dietl to withdraw overland south to the port of Trondheim, since Narvik could not be held. Another said he should evacuate by air. A third order instructed Dietl to retreat eastward along the railroad leading to the Swedish border. None of the orders reached Dietl, however. They were quietly intercepted by General Jodl, OKW chief of operations, who complained in his diary that Hitler had created "chaos in the command system" with his stream of "orders in every detail." Jodl attempted to calm the Führer. "A thing should be considered lost," he told Hitler, "only when it is actually lost."

Hitler grew more reasonable. On April 18, he approved an order instructing Dietl to hold Narvik as long as possible before withdrawing into the interior. But a Luftwaffe intelligence report that British troop transports were in the vicinity of Trondheim plunged Hitler into despair. At the Reich Chancellery, Warlimont recalled, the Führer sat "hunched in a chair in the corner, unnoticed and staring in front of him, a picture of brooding gloom. He appeared to be waiting for some piece of news that would save the situation." Yet when the campaign eventually succeeded after six weeks of hard fighting, Hitler forgot his vacillations and fears. Victory came, he said, "because there was a man like me, who did not know the word *impossible*."

His reputation now higher than ever, Hitler pushed forward energetically with plans for the assault on the West. Here he showed considerable flexibility. He grew dissatisfied with his original scheme, which emphasized the northern flank of the front, because it repeated the opening phases of the German offensive of 1914. It was unlikely to surprise the Allies, and it committed the bulk of the armored divisions to the Low Countries, where innumerable rivers and canals made maneuver difficult. As an alternative, he pondered shifting the weight of the attack elsewhere. His top generals also favored a different approach and, after considerable study, produced a daring plan. Their idea was to move the main attack south and focus it on the Forest of Ardennes, in southern Belgium. German armor would attack through the Ardennes, cross the Meuse River between Dinant and Sedan, and knife across the rolling terrain of northern France to the English Channel near the mouth of the Somme. The victorious German forces would then swing north to encircle the British and French armies advancing to meet a secondary German attack in the Low Countries. The great merit of the plan was surprise; the Ardennes, because of its craggy, densely wooded hills and twisting roads, was thought to be almost impenetrable to armored forces, and, accordingly, French defenses were weakest in that sector.

The scheme was also dangerous. If the Ardennes proved more difficult than expected and the Allies were able to mount a counterattack, Hitler's offensive would founder. Hitler understood the risk, but the plan appealed to his taste for daring and surprise, and he did not hesitate to approve it.

During the forty-six-day campaign that began on May 10, Hitler was elated time after time by a dazzling string of victories. In the company of the OKW staff, he followed the action from Felsennest, or Rocky Refuge, a bunker complex blasted out of a wooded hilltop in far western Germany, near the borders of Belgium and Holland. When German troops overran Dutch and Belgian defenses and burst into the Belgian plains, he could hardly contain his joy. Hitler himself had overseen the planning of glider and paratroop attacks to seize key bridges before they could be destroyed. And it had been Hitler's idea to capture the formidable Belgian fort of Eben

Emael by landing troop-carrying gliders on its broad roof. His endorsement of the gamble in the Ardennes was triumphantly vindicated on May 13. That day, German armor crossed the Meuse and smashed through the French Second and Ninth Armies. Jodl noted in his diary that Hitler was "beside himself with joy" and even had good words for the leaders of the German army when the advance units of General Heinz Guderian's panzer corps reached the Channel coast on May 20, cutting the Allied forces in two.

Even in this brilliantly executed campaign, Hitler showed himself to be a commander plagued by doubt. Despite his stated belief in speed and mobility, he grew wary of counterattacks that could snap his extended lines and frantically ordered the panzer divisions to halt on a number of occasions. "Führer is terribly nervous," wrote Halder in his diary a week after the

At Felsennest in May 1940, Hitler pores over a report on the fighting in France while attended by his military commanders— Admiral Erich Raeder *(with hand in pocket)* and General Wilhelm Keitel. At right, the simple furnishings of Hitler's quarters reflect his determination to set a Spartan example for the troops.

A Failed Flight for Peace

On May 11, 1941, two adjutants arrived at the Berghof with an urgent letter from Rudolf Hess. A few moments later, those waiting outside the Führer's study heard an "inarticulate, almost animal outcry." To his utter rage, Adolf Hitler had just learned that Hess, his trusted deputy, had flown to Scotland.

Increasingly overshadowed in the Nazi hierarchy by his deputy, Martin Bormann, Hess for some time had harbored the notion that he might regain the Führer's favor by enlisting Germany's "Aryan blood brothers," the British, in the coming war with bolshevism. His first effort in this direction consisted of a letter written during the au-

tumn of 1940 to the Duke of Hamilton, whom he had met at the Berlin Olympics in 1936. Receiving no reply, he decided to fly directly to the duke's country estate in Scotland.

His plans were laid with care. An accomplished pilot, he persuaded Willy Messerschmitt, the aircraft designer, to loan him an Me 110 fighter for a series of practice flights. Hess fitted the plane with auxiliary gas tanks and a special radio and took off from Augsburg, in Bavaria, on the afternoon of May 10. He navigated so well that after a flight of 800 miles, he parachuted only 12 miles from the duke's home.

Both Hess's aircraft and his hopes for Aryan fraternity were

dashed in the United Kingdom. Neither the duke nor the British officials who interviewed him were interested in his peace plan. Instead, he was interned in the Tower of London as a prisoner of war.

In Berlin, days of panicky speculation and prickly embarrassment followed Hess's defection, but tension subsided when it became apparent that, for all his naiveté, Hess had not given up any secrets about the imminent surprise attack on Russia. Bormann, indulging his appetite for power, expunged Hess's name from party records and monuments, removed his picture from public places, and slithered into place as Hitler's new secretary.

Before a practice flight, Rudolf Hess *(left)* stands in the cockpit of the Me 110 he flew on a peace mission to Britain in May 1941.

Even though Hitler had forbidden him to fly during the war, Hess, who believed in astrology, dreamed about flying on an important mission over water. If his quest failed, Hess wrote to Hitler, "Simply say I am crazy."

Scottish troops inspect the wreckage of Hess's fighter *(below)*. Unable to find a landing place, Hess bailed out and allowed the plane to crash.

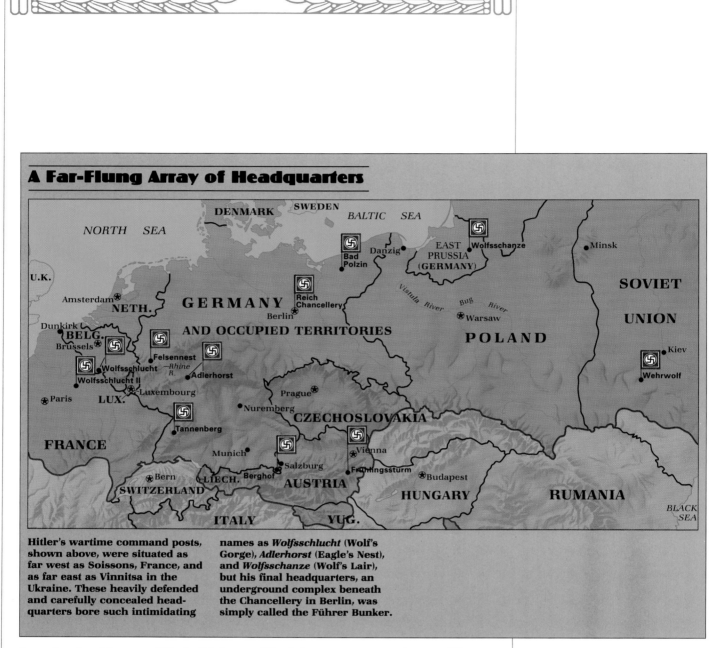

A Far-Flung Array of Headquarters

Hitler's wartime command posts, shown above, were situated as far west as Soissons, France, and as far east as Vinnitsa in the Ukraine. These heavily defended and carefully concealed headquarters bore such intimidating names as *Wolfsschlucht* (Wolf's Gorge), *Adlerhorst* (Eagle's Nest), and *Wolfsschanze* (Wolf's Lair), but his final headquarters, an underground complex beneath the Chancellery in Berlin, was simply called the Führer Bunker.

invasion had begun. "He is frightened by his own success, is unwilling to take any risks, and is trying to hold us back." A day later, Halder found Hitler still "full of incomprehensible fear. He rages and shouts that we are doing our best to ruin the entire operation. He entirely refuses to carry on the operation westward." At Felsennest, in a wooden hut used as a briefing room, Hitler pored over maps far into the night, sporadically firing off orders and counterorders. His panzer commanders became so frustrated that, in some sectors, they continued the advance without authorization.

None of Hitler's decisions was more controversial than his order to halt the armored advance just short of Dunkirk. The pause allowed the remnants of the French and British forces to evacuate the port and escape across the Channel to England. He gave several explanations. One was that he wanted to conserve the depleted armored formations, half of whose tanks were at least temporarily out of service, for the coming battle for Paris and southern France. Then, too, Göring had argued forcefully that the Luftwaffe alone could destroy the retreating enemy. Hitler even suggested that the decision to halt was a political one—a gesture of clemency that he expected would lead to a rapid truce with Britain. Whatever the reasons, the tanks stood motionless before Dunkirk for nearly three days, until Hitler realized the Luftwaffe could not stop the British evacuation. When the panzers returned to the attack, it was too late; more than 300,000 Allied troops had escaped to fight another day.

Nevertheless, the campaign had been brilliant, and when France laid down its arms three weeks later, Hitler's estimate of himself as the "greatest strategic genius of all time" seemed correct. Several of his underlings believed so. "And wherein lies the secret of this victory?" gushed the former skeptic, Brigadier General Eduard Wagner. "Indeed, in the enormous dynamism of the Führer. Without his will, it would never have come to pass."

In fact, Hitler had again displayed an exceptional grasp of strategy and a flair for technical detail. But to those who worked with him, it was obvious that he did not have the temperament for the day-by-day operation of a military campaign. He was too excitable, too changeable, too reluctant to delegate authority, and too ready to blame others for his own mistakes. When operations in the field did not go as he expected, he often panicked. Subjected to the stress of battle, he lacked the "nerves of iron" that he frequently boasted were his greatest strength.

Victories in the west dangerously bolstered Hitler's opinion of his own capabilities. "This little affair of operational command," he said, "is something anybody can do." He also compounded his shortcomings by shunning his generals. His commanders offered advice reluctantly, or not at all, because he routinely denied them access to adequate information. This way, he curtailed their power and enhanced his own. For instance, Hitler had foreign-office intelligence kept from the high command and military intelligence withheld from the foreign office. "No one was told more than the Führer wanted him to know," Keitel remarked. Moreover, many in his entourage were determined to shield him—to preserve his "sleepwalker's sense of security," as Speer said—while others were afraid to confront him. Even forceful commanders became "insignificant and timid" in Hitler's presence, Speer observed. "When I confront this man," confessed Brauchitsch, "I feel as if someone were choking me, and I cannot find another word." Field Marshal Erhard Milch recalled facing Hitler "like a very small boy who has not done his sums properly." Admiral Karl Dönitz avoided Hitler: "I purposely went very seldom to his headquarters, for I had the feeling that I would thus best preserve my power of initiative, and also because after several days there, I felt that I must disengage myself from his power of suggestion." Those who withstood the power enough to sound a note of criticism were accused of lacking the "spirit of the Reich Chancellery," which recognized only "boldness."

Perhaps more crippling than any of these defects was Hitler's lack of knowledge about his foreign enemies. Although he had an uncanny knack for detecting their weaknesses—as when he assured his generals that France would not attack in the west while he was demolishing Poland—he was blinded by biases and preconceptions based on trivial data. The film *The Grapes of Wrath*, for example, led him to discount America's fighting ability; instead of a strong rural population, he believed, the country had only "miserable and degenerate farmers" wandering about in a "completely uprooted mob." He based a similarly distorted appraisal of the Russians' fighting capacity on muddled notions of Slavic racial inferiority dating from his student days. His estimate of the British was in some ways more realistic, but in others just as flawed. He respected them as members of a fellow Nordic nation but could not understand their reluctance to stand with Germany against their mutual enemy, bolshevism. After his triumph in France, Hitler was probably sincere when he proclaimed that he saw no reason why Germany's war with Britain need go on.

The misguided hope that he could sign a separate peace no doubt contributed to his hesitancy to launch a cross-Channel invasion in the summer of 1940. He mulled over seven possible operations, ranging from an invasion of Britain to the support of the Italians in North Africa and an attack on the Soviet Union. Why he decided against an invasion of the British Isles is unclear. The dominance of the Royal Navy and the Luftwaffe's failure to establish air supremacy over England certainly had much to do with it. So did his fear of rising Soviet strength and his conviction that Britain would be forced to come to terms if he dispatched Russia quickly. He regarded war with the Soviet Union as inevitable: In seeking new living space, he had written in *Mein Kampf*, Germany could "think primarily only of Russia and its vast vassal border states." His decision to attack in the east before he had conquered Britain marked the turning point of the war.

Before he committed his forces to the Russian invasion, however, Hitler had to shore up the flagging fortunes of his Axis partner, Italy. Germany's lightning conquests of Yugoslavia and Greece in April 1941 and of Crete in May not only saved the Italians from the consequences of their inept Greek invasion but greatly added to Hitler's aura of infallibility. His further decision to dispatch German mechanized forces to North Africa under General Erwin Rommel during April resulted in quick defeat for the British, who retreated toward Egypt. With these strokes, Hitler restored the initiative to the Axis powers. But they were only preliminaries to the invasion of the Soviet Union on June 22, 1941—a campaign that would test the supreme commander's powers of leadership as never before.

If Hitler had sought the opinion of his generals, he would have discovered that they gravely doubted the army's readiness for such a formidable challenge. Moreover, they were skeptical of his proposed plan of operations. All agreed on a three-pronged offensive to destroy the Soviet armies west of the Dvina and Dnieper rivers before they could retreat into the vast Russian interior. But the high command thought this could be best accomplished by giving the weight of the armor to Army Group Center for a concentrated drive on Moscow, which, as the capital and the country's western communications center, would inevitably have to be defended by the bulk of the Soviet armies. Hitler, on the other hand, dismissed Moscow as "merely a geographical idea." He insisted instead on stripping Army Group Center of its mobile forces to reinforce two huge flanking operations—one toward Leningrad and the Baltic in the north and the other to the south, toward the agricultural and industrial riches of the Donets Basin and the Ukraine. Only after these objectives had been attained would the army groups in the north and south swing inward to converge on Moscow.

To military leaders, Hitler's plan was confused in its aims and reckless in its dispersal of forces across huge distances. But Hitler had his eye on the booty he needed to keep his war machine going: "My generals," he snapped, "know nothing about a war economy." The high command was not converted, and disagreement about strategic objectives would haunt the campaign. When his armies crossed the Russian frontier, Hitler moved his permanent headquarters to the Forest of Görlitz, just east of Rastenburg in East Prussia, and gave it the code name *Wolfsschanze*, or Wolf's Lair. Here he would remain until November 20, 1944. He made only occasional forays to field headquarters such as Wehrwolf, near Vinnitsa in the Ukraine, and rare visits to Berlin or the Berghof, his mountain retreat in Bavaria. He had not anticipated the long stay at Wolfsschanze, for he expected victory over Russia in three months. "We have only to kick in the door," he told Jodl, "and the whole rotten structure will come crashing down."

At first, the optimism seemed justified. The German advance was so rapid—400 miles in the first three weeks—and the Soviet armies so demoralized and shattered that Halder wrote in his diary, "The campaign has been won in fourteen days." Hitler, too, told his entourage that "the Russians have lost the war" and issued a directive calling for a reduction in army strength and a corresponding expansion of the Luftwaffe for the coming campaign against Britain.

At this critical juncture, Hitler's generals renewed their pleas for a de-

At left, the outline of a bunker is discernible in the woods at Wolfsschanze, Hitler's command center in East Prussia. Below, protected by concrete walls, telephone operators handle calls from the Russian front. The operators were forbidden to eavesdrop on the conversations.

cisive thrust toward Moscow, barely 200 miles away. Hitler turned them down. Intoxicated by success and blinded by the urge to win everything at once, he ordered Army Group Center to hold fast against increasingly violent counterattacks while he diverted its armor to Army Groups North and South. Then he sent the two wings of the thousand-mile front fanning out in pursuit of ever more distant goals. The great battle of Kiev, in which Field Marshal Gerd von Rundstedt's reinforced Army Group South captured 665,000 Russian soldiers, seemed once again to confirm Hitler's military genius, but it was largely a tactical victory, and it consumed valuable time.

It was September before Hitler consented to a general advance on Moscow, and even then he could not focus on one objective. Field Marshal Wilhelm von Leeb's Army Group North was ordered at the same time to take Leningrad, while Rundstedt's Army Group South was to clear the Crimean peninsula and strike beyond Rostov to the Volga River and the oil fields of the Caucasus. "We laughed aloud when we received these orders," recalled Rundstedt—winter had come and the objectives were 400 miles away. The weather doomed the Moscow offensive almost before it began: In the snow and the sub-zero cold of December, Hitler's forces halted before the Soviet capital. Brauchitsch resigned, and Hitler announced that he was taking over the functions of the army commander in chief himself.

As was his practice, Hitler blamed his commanding general for the setback. Joseph Goebbels, after a visit to Hitler's headquarters, noted in his diary that "the Führer spoke of Brauchitsch only in terms of contempt—a vain, cowardly wretch who could not even appraise the situation, much less master it. By his constant interference and consistent disobedience, he completely spoiled the entire plan for the eastern campaign as it was designed with crystal clarity by the Führer." Henceforth, Hitler immersed himself almost totally in the day-by-day direction of the war on the eastern

At a forward airfield in the Ukraine, Adolf Hitler and Benito Mussolini share an alfresco meal with officers of Army Group South in the late summer of 1941. At Mussolini's right is Field Marshal Gerd von Rundstedt, whom Hitler would soon fire in a dispute over strategy.

front. When the Russians launched a massive counteroffensive, he ignored his generals' pleas for a tactical withdrawal and insisted that the German armies stand fast through the Russian winter. "A general withdrawal is out of the question," he ordered. "The idea that we should prepare rear positions is just driveling nonsense." The Germans lost many men and much equipment to both the enemy and the cold—most of the troops did without winter clothing because Hitler had insisted the campaign would be over by fall—but they eventually beat back the Russian attack. In the spring, they were still deep in Russia and ready to resume the offensive.

In the summer of 1942, when Hitler got his armies moving again, he made his principal drive on the southern flank. The objectives were Stalingrad, the vital industrial center, and the Caucasus oil fields, which he felt he must have to sustain the war. From his temporary headquarters in the Ukraine, Hitler watched with mounting excitement as his armies raced down the corridor between the Don and Donets rivers, convinced again that victory was within his grasp. Although the advance in the Caucasus was rapid, it took the Germans only to the edge of the oil fields before they outran their supply lines and Soviet resistance stiffened. At Stalingrad, units of General Friedrich von Paulus's Sixth Army took positions north and south of the city but by early September could progress no farther. When Halder, chief of the army high command, recommended that the attack be broken off, he, too, was relieved. What was needed now, said Hitler, was not professional ability but "National Socialist ardor." To replace Halder, he named Lieut. General Kurt Zeitzler, a younger and more optimistic officer.

Halder feared that Hitler's underestimation of the enemy was "assuming grotesque forms." Told that the Soviets could muster a million additional men in the region north of Stalingrad and that their tank production had reached 1,200 a month, the Führer erupted in rage, shouting that he did not want to hear "such idiotic nonsense." The isolation of his headquarters reinforced his tendency to reject bad news. Wolfsschanze, to which Hitler returned in November, struck Jodl as a "mixture of cloister and concentration camp. Apart from reports on the military situation, very little news from the outside world penetrated into this holy of holies." Minefields and barbed wire encircled the complex, which was hidden by trees and scarcely visible from the nearest road. Hitler and his entourage worked in wooden huts surrounding a central barracks where most of the staff lived. Hitler moved into a massive bunker that was impervious to bombs and sunlight. There, beneath fifteen feet of concrete, he occupied a suite of three small rooms with undecorated walls and bare wooden furniture. He claimed to want no amenities not available to the front-line soldier.

The main focus of the day was the noon briefing. Present with assorted adjutants and liaison officers were Keitel and Jodl; the chief of staff of the army; representatives of the Luftwaffe, navy, and foreign office; and sometimes Heinrich Himmler, Göring, or Speer. They all stood around a large map table except for Hitler, who sat in a plain armchair with a rush seat. Göring, too, was permitted to sit, in deference to his bulk. As maps were spread out and the situation in various theaters reported, Hitler asked questions, weighed possibilities, and made—or deferred—decisions. The stenographic records of the conferences that have survived show him at times to have been shrewd and incisive, but more often meandering and absorbed in trivia. Occasional serious strategic analyses were mixed with lectures on the treatment of guerrilla forces or the dangers of leaving a soldier in the front lines too long. What struck Speer was the range of problems that Hitler presumed himself fit to resolve. The Führer was mainly interested in the eastern front, but he was also involved in the affairs of occupied Europe, the political and military fortunes of the Italians, and the German campaign in Africa, where Rommel's latest offensive had stalled at the Egyptian border.

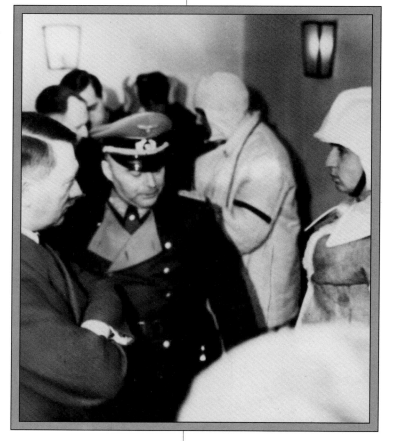

In a typical day, a second, more restricted conference might take place in late afternoon, followed by dinner between eight o'clock and midnight. Hitler usually ate with his staff in the officers' mess, a dreary pine-board shack that reminded Speer of a "railroad-station restaurant in a small town." The insomniac Hitler harangued his captive audience and prolonged the meal as late as he could. He usually ended his day drinking tea with his secretaries at four in the morning. At first, they listened to recordings of Ludwig van Beethoven, Richard Wagner, and Hugo Wolf, but as the war news worsened, Hitler lost his taste for music and spent hours reminiscing about the past. His only recreation consisted of morning walks with his German shepherd, Blondi.

In late 1942 and early 1943, major reverses on the battlefield plagued Hitler. In Africa, the British defeated Rommel at El Alamein, and soon thereafter Allied troops landed on the coast of Algeria and occupied all of French North Africa to the Tunisian border. At Stalingrad, three Russian army groups encircled the embattled Sixth Army, which was so hard-

Hitler inspects soldiers modeling cold-weather gear in 1942. Failure to provide German troops in Russia with adequate clothing the previous winter resulted in untold suffering and 113,000 cases of frostbite.

pressed that Paulus asked repeatedly for permission to break out to the southwest. Hitler persistently refused. After the success of his no-retreat policy the winter before, he had forbidden commanders to execute even a minor tactical withdrawal without his approval. The order was taken seriously; officers on the Russian front quipped that a battalion commander dared not move a sentry from the window to the door.

To the desperate Paulus, Hitler cabled that withdrawal and surrender were equally unthinkable: "The Sixth Army will do its historic duty at Stalingrad until the last man." When Paulus nevertheless surrendered on January 31, 1943, Hitler took it as a betrayal. In a staff conference, he said that he could not understand why Paulus had not committed suicide rather than surrender. "When you think that a woman has sufficient pride, just because someone has made a few insulting remarks, to go and lock herself in and shoot herself right off, then I've no respect for a soldier who is afraid to do that but would rather be taken prisoner," Hitler raged. "I can't understand why a man like Paulus wouldn't rather die. The heroism of so many tens of thousands of men, officers, and generals is canceled out by a man like this who hasn't the character, when the moment comes, to do what a weakling of a woman can do."

Hitler's isolation now became even more intense. Refusing to eat with his staff officers, he took all his meals in his rooms. He gave only two more major speeches in public after Stalingrad, and his annual Munich celebration speech was read for him in his absence. As bad fortune continued to befall him, he ceased issuing the war directives that had defined his strategic and political goals during his days of triumph. At the same time, he told his staff to suspend all long-range planning studies, which could come only to conclusions that he refused to accept.

Rather than travel to Germany's bombed and blackened cities, he summoned dignitaries to Wolfsschanze or even to his headquarters in the Ukraine. A trip to the Russian outpost involved three days of train travel for a brief, often irrelevant chat with the Führer. Shortly after Stalingrad, Hitler explained to a delegation of gauleiters and reichsleiters that cowardly conscript Rumanian and Hungarian formations in the German battle line were responsible for the disaster. For the privilege of more frequent contact with Hitler, ministers such as Joachim von Ribbentrop, Göring, and Himmler set up nearby satellite headquarters that reminded one visitor of the "imperial camps of the seventeenth and eighteenth centuries, when princes and their courts followed in the wake of their armies."

As Germany's military fortunes shifted, so did the balance of power in the Nazi hierarchy. The bizarre departure of Rudolf Hess for Scotland in the

spring of 1941 left a vacancy that Hess's assistant, Martin Bormann, quickly filled. Hess's post of deputy führer was abolished, but Bormann gathered the reins of the party into his own hands as head of a newly created Party Chancellery. With the mixture of diligence and fanatical zeal that was typical of him, he set out to develop a power base from which to undermine his rivals and vault to the top of Hitler's inner circle. His two great weapons were his authority over the gauleiters, who could not be appointed without his approval, and his access to Hitler. The gauleiters had been given new responsibility for civil defense in their districts, and this in turn put Bormann in effective control of the entire civilian war effort. But he wanted more than that and got it after he was designated secretary to the Führer in the spring of 1943. Bormann now claimed the right to range into areas far beyond the normal jurisdiction of the party. His heavy hand was felt on the courts, the churches, the prisoner-of-war program, matters of internal security, and the functioning of the state bureaucracy. Although he theoretically shared with Himmler command of the home guard known as the Volkssturm, he, in fact, was the dominant partner.

Bormann decided who would see Hitler and when, and he did not hesitate to bar high-ranking generals or ministers. No matter was too trifling or too great for Bormann's attention. He took care of Hitler's personal finances, selected most of his reading material, obtained food for his special diet, and entertained him with an assiduously built collection of jokes about the leading Nazis. At the same time, he suggested to Hitler, or wrote himself, many of the Führer directives that defined domestic policy in the later years of the war. The grateful Hitler declared Bormann indispensable and referred to him as "my most loyal party comrade."

In what time he could spare from waiting on Hitler, Bormann, a fanatical anti-Christian, led a campaign against the churches. He also pushed for the most extreme measures in the treatment of Jews, Slavs, and prisoners of war. As the self-appointed guardian of party "purity," he encouraged the gauleiters to circumvent the courts and dispense their own brand of justice in cases of suspected disloyalty. Under his vigilant eye, people were beheaded or shot for defeatist remarks or for neglecting to say, "Heil Hitler!" By 1943, this short, squat bureaucrat, whose name and face were scarcely known to the German public, had become the most powerful man in the Reich after Hitler himself, and perhaps the most feared.

There was one man he could not touch, however, and that was Alfred Speer. A gifted technician and planner, Speer enjoyed an independence shared by no one else in the Nazi hierarchy. The architect took over as Reich minister for armaments and war production in 1942, succeeding Fritz Todt, who had been killed in a plane crash. Against all odds, Speer

Above, Hitler and other elite Nazis attend the 1929 wedding of Martin Bormann and Gerda Buch. At far left is Rudolf Hess, whom Bormann would replace as the aide closest to Hitler.

Holding her youngest child, Gerda Bormann lines up seven others by height and age for a wartime snapshot. Although Martin Bormann worried about the children's safety during the war, he was also a tyrannical father who often whipped them for minor transgressions.

A top-hatted temptress in the style of Marlene Dietrich, Manja Behrens *(right)* poses for a photo publicizing one of her movies, a film called *Susanna Bathing*.

A Boastful Philanderer

Hitler's private secretary, Martin Bormann, was as energetic, egotistical, and overbearing with the women in his life as he was when pursuing political power. Married to tall, handsome Gerda Buch, the daughter of an important early Nazi official, Bormann kept his wife steadily pregnant with a succession of ten children. Yet he was a domestic boor, treating his spouse like a lackey, ordering her about and insulting her in front of guests. "He behaved toward his wife," reported fellow Nazi Walther Darré, "the way you'd expect some uncouth bum from the slums to carry on."

Bormann also betrayed her by indulging in affair after affair. In 1943, he took as his mistress the stage and film actress Manja Behrens, who was a friend of his wife. After his first night with Manja, Bormann wrote Gerda a letter describing the seduction in detail and boasting, "I took her in spite of her refusals. You know my will power; in the long run, M. just could not resist." He solemnly added that he would henceforth stay in good physical shape so that his sexual powers would suffice for two women.

Even this did not drive his wife away. In fact, she invited Behrens to stay in the Bormann home and kept in touch with her after her husband, tiring of the affair, abruptly dumped his mistress. "Even among so many ruthless men," wrote Albert Speer, Bormann "stood out by his brutality and coarseness."

increased the output of German factories even as German cities were reduced to rubble and eastern industrial and mining regions were lost to the advancing Soviet armies. Incredibly, German aircraft and munitions production reached an all-time high just ten months before the end of the war. In 1944, Germany produced seven times as many weapons as in 1942, five times as many armored vehicles, and six times as much ammunition. Yet the labor force had increased by only 30 percent.

To work these miracles, Speer first had to restore some measure of order to a production system fragmented by conflicting demands and internal rivalries. Defense plants of the army, navy, and Luftwaffe were competing for labor and raw materials with factories largely run by the gauleiters, and all those were vying with plants run by Himmler and the SS. So many different agencies were in charge of procurement, Speer warned a meeting of gauleiters, that their orders for copper exceeded the world's supply.

Speer relied on his high standing with Hitler, who gave him virtual carte blanche to run all German industry, with the exception of the SS plants. Thus empowered, Speer announced a program of "industrial self-responsibility." Plants that had been turning out armaments piecemeal, more or less on demand, geared up for mass production. For greater efficiency, a factory would now produce only one kind of item, not several as before. Plant managers received full responsibility for the performance of their factories, free of coercion by party or state. Speer encouraged improvisation and a free flow of information between factories and re-

Hitler questions his armaments minister, Albert Speer *(far left)*, while inspecting an improved model of an armored vehicle in December 1942. Hitler relished such occasions as opportunities to show off his store of memorized technical facts.

Albert Speer, recently appointed minister of armaments and war production, test-drives an experimental tank up a muddy slope at the Henschel works in Kassel in 1942. The VK 3601(H) prototype was a forerunner of the formidable Tiger tank.

warded initiative and constructive criticism. When the Gestapo tried to arrest three of his managers for "defeatist" conversations, he protected them by insisting that the necessities of war production made candid assessments of the situation essential. Beyond this, he fought to keep his deliberately loose organizational structure from becoming a bureaucracy. When the ministry's files burned in an air raid, he welcomed the loss of "useless ballast" but warned his colleagues not to count on such fortuitous raids to "continually introduce the necessary fresh air into our work."

Speer hired anybody who could do the job—his ministry was a nest of antiparty sentiment, Bormann charged angrily—and he shared none of the gauleiters' reluctance to use the detested "inferior" peoples, such as Slavs

or Hungarian Jews, on the assembly line. Accordingly, he competed constantly with Himmler for workers. By 1943, foreigners (volunteers or forced laborers, concentration-camp inmates, and prisoners of war) made up 40 percent of the 14 million workers in Speer's war factories. In general, he was in favor of decent working conditions and adequate food for the slave labor he employed, but not for humanitarian reasons: He had simply observed that production fell when his workers were starved and exhausted.

Of the older leaders of Hitler's Reich, only four—Göring, Ribbentrop, Himmler, and Goebbels—were much in evidence by the middle of the war. While the last two retained genuine power and even augmented it, Göring and Ribbentrop had become mere figureheads. The Reich marshal still had an impressive panoply of titles—commander in chief of the Luftwaffe, plenipotentiary for the Four-Year Plan, president of the Reichstag, and many others—but he had been virtually written off by Hitler, who confided to Speer that he knew Göring was corrupt and a drug addict. The failure of his Luftwaffe to supply the Sixth Army at Stalingrad, following on the failure of its aerial assault on England, apparently finished Göring in Hitler's eyes. Now, when Göring appeared in public wearing one of his white or sky blue

SS chief Heinrich Himmler *(center),* accompanied by Arthur Axmann, leader of the Hitler Youth, inspects the new 12th SS Panzer Division, recruited in 1943 from the ranks of the Hitler Youth. Himmler, said the Führer, is training "young men who will make the world tremble."

uniforms and bearing his bejeweled marshal's baton, he was likely to be treated as a figure of fun and heckled about his boast in 1939 that not one enemy bomber would ever cross the German frontier. As Allied bombing increased, Hitler berated him openly and violently. In response, Göring withdrew more and more to his palatial estate, Karinhall, where he hunted, feasted, and added to his collection of plundered artworks and jewels.

Joachim von Ribbentrop tried to keep up the pretense of power, but he spent so much time defending his prerogatives, noted a colleague, that he had no time for anything else. Although he still occupied the post of foreign minister, the Führer rarely consulted him. Nevertheless, Ribbentrop passed most of his time at his field headquarters near Hitler, waiting to be summoned while much of the work of his ministry went undone. "A single frown from Führer headquarters," observed Ribbentrop's press chief, "and his whole world tumbles about the ears."

Himmler, meanwhile, consolidated his position as one of the most sinister forces of the Reich. Already in control of the police state's vast machinery of political oppression as chief of the SS and the Gestapo, he extended his power over the civil service and the courts after Hitler named him minister of the interior in 1943. His domain included not only the concentration camps, which he used as a source of labor for his SS factories, but also the extermination camps, where he developed systems of mass murder to eliminate "racial degenerates" such as Slavs and Jews. By 1944, he had taken over from the army responsibility for military intelligence and prisoner-of-war camps and controlled political administration in the occupied territories in the east. His Waffen-SS, numbering half a million men, acted like a private army. Late in the war, he was even given command of an army group on the eastern front, despite his lack of military experience. Although he bored Hitler, who found him pedantic, he had put together a realm of power that constituted almost a state within a state.

Goebbels, more realistic than Himmler, was the first of the Nazi leaders to sense that the tide was turning against Germany. Failing to persuade Hitler to consider a compromise peace, he threw all his energy into galvanizing the public for the total war he proclaimed in a rousing speech at the Sportpalast just after the Stalingrad disaster. The Allies' demand for unconditional surrender, he asserted, meant that Germans had to choose between victory and destruction. Shrewdly playing on the panic, pathos, blind faith, and self-delusion he sensed in the public mood, he mixed apocalyptic visions of "Asiatic hordes" with morale-boosting hints of German secret weapons and impregnable fortresses in the mountains. He even contrived favorable astrological forecasts and planted them in the press, explaining to his aides that "crazy times call for crazy measures."

Because Hitler was no longer visible, Goebbels became more than ever the voice and the presence of the regime. He alone among Nazi leaders visited the bombed ruins of German cities. When Hitler named him plenipotentiary for total war in 1944, Goebbels forced the closing of many luxury shops and restaurants and campaigned against the high-living party elite and war profiteers the public referred to derisively as the Golden Pheasants. Although nothing delighted him more than shutting Horcher's, Göring's favorite Berlin restaurant, he also tried, unsuccessfully, to resurrect Göring's reputation to balance Bormann's ominously growing power. Domestic policy, warned Goebbels, had slipped entirely out of Hitler's hands. "Things cannot go on this way," he told Speer.

Yet things continued to go on that way; Goebbels's efforts to persuade the Führer to spend more time in Berlin met with little success. Having decreed that 1943 was to be the "year of clenched teeth," Hitler declared that his place was near his soldiers. At his headquarters, Speer found him a changed man. "Earlier, he had made decisions with almost sportive ease," recalled Speer. "Now he had to force them out of his exhausted brain." Early in 1943, Hitler's associates noticed the trembling of his left arm and leg that would last the rest of his life. In order to restore his flagging energies and combat his bouts of depression, he relied on narcotics and stimulants that were given him by Dr. Theodor Morell, the quack physician introduced to him by his photographer.

At left, an overflow audience at the Berlin Sportpalast—including the wounded veterans with their nurses shown at right—hears Propaganda Minister Joseph Goebbels call for "total war" in a watershed address after the German defeat at Stalingrad. Hitler failed to attend, but he later called the speech a "psychological masterpiece."

What surprised Speer was not that Hitler was a shadow of his former self but that he could function at all. In February 1943, the Führer roused himself enough to fly to the Ukraine, his last visit to a war front. Ostensibly, he went there to take charge of his hard-pressed Army Group South, which was being driven from the Donets Basin. In this critical situation, Hitler told the troops that the "fate of Germany's present and future" was in their hands and promised them "more and more divisions" and "weapons unique and hitherto unknown." In fact, Hitler did make one positive move: He gave a free hand to Army Group South's brilliant commander, General Erich von Manstein, and found reinforcements for him. As a result, Manstein engineered a counteroffensive that recaptured the Donets Basin and the key city of Kharkov and stabilized the German lines.

Characteristically, Hitler took all the credit. According to Warlimont, "Hitler returned to East Prussia from the Ukraine with the air of a victorious warlord, clearly considering himself and his leadership primarily responsible for the favorable turn of events in the east. The real organizer of this victory was Manstein." Back in Berlin, the offensive was hailed as the "miracle on the Donets," but it was to be one of the Wehrmacht's last successes. In early May, the fall of Tunis and Bizerte to the Allies and the subsequent surrender of all Axis forces in North Africa shook Hitler. In July came the Allied conquest of Sicily and the fall of Mussolini's government. Cool in this crisis, Hitler swiftly dispatched German reinforcements to Italy, where they seized control of the government and deployed to meet the Allied landings in September.

In Russia, where Hitler's leadership was being most severely tested, the news was almost all bad. Against the advice of most of his generals, he ordered a major offensive on the central front in July, employing half a million of his finest troops, including seventeen panzer divisions. The Russian lines bent but held, and they responded along the whole front with an attack that pushed the Germans back, past the scenes of their triumphs, toward the Polish and Rumanian frontiers. It was clear, noted Speer, that "even in the summer, the initiative had passed to the enemy."

Forced to fight a defensive war, Hitler found his strategic options limited to deciding which towns to defend against an avalanche of Soviet tanks and infantry. In some sectors, the Russians outnumbered the Germans by seven to one. He was learning all too well the truth of one of his own observations: "It's a thousand times easier to storm forward with an army and gain victories than to bring an army back in an orderly condition after a reverse or defeat." Yet Hitler continued to insist that the most minor tactical decisions be referred to him. "I cannot leave military decisions to others, even for twenty-four hours," he complained bitterly.

As the Soviets reached the Polish frontier and Allied forces fought northward on the Italian peninsula in the winter of 1944, those around Hitler noticed his increasing refusal to look at the threatening realities of the world outside his bunker. He dismissed reliable figures on American aircraft production and Soviet war potential as sheer propaganda. He insisted that Winston Churchill was an incompetent alcoholic and that Franklin D. Roosevelt suffered not from infantile paralysis, but syphilitic paralysis, and

Hitler watches Blondi, his Alsatian, leap over hurdles during their morning walk within the confines of Wolfsschanze. Hitler was devoted to the dog; according to an aide, Blondi "probably meant more to the Führer than his closest associates."

hence was mentally unsound. When planning strategy, he invariably computed at full strength German army units that had all but ceased to exist. Captive to his theory that democracy enfeebled a nation, he predicted that Allied troops would break and run in their first serious encounter. When the Allies landed in Normandy in June of 1944, he refused to believe Rommel and Rundstedt, who maintained that the enemy could not be thrown back into the sea. All his generals were cowards and liars who fed him deliberately unfavorable information, Hitler ranted, "to force me to authorize retreats."

What kept him going was his undiminished self-confidence and faith in his mission. "He was by nature a religious man," observed Speer, "but his capacity for belief had been perverted into belief in himself." Speer was convinced that, if there was any "fundamental insanity" in Hitler, it was this "unshakable belief in his lucky star." In fact, Speer and many others near Hitler in the last desperate months of the war found the Führer's conviction and personal magnetism so strong that he was still able to convince them almost against their will that victory was possible. Even the cynical Goebbels came back from Führer headquarters exuding an optimism that violated his sense of the facts. Goebbels's press officer marveled at the strength that enabled Hitler, "with a look and a handshake," to change the opinion of a "sober, realistic man such as myself."

People beyond Hitler's direct influence had no illusions, however. As it became clear not only that the war was lost but that Hitler intended to fight to the bitter end and drag Germany down with him, the spirit of revolt gained a new impetus. Now, if ever, was the time to overthrow the leader who had wasted the nation and brought it to the brink of defeat. ✚

The Man of 1,000 Costumes

egarding matters of dress, Hitler's inner circle tended to drabness, but Hermann Göring was an ever-dazzling exception. Imbued with Teutonic romanticism and a flair for the dramatic, he strutted across the stage of the Third Reich vividly costumed for whatever his role of the moment required. At his sumptuous lodge, Karinhall, he became the country squire shown on these two pages, donning an array of Alpine-style leather jerkins and breeches, bright tunics, knee-high boots, feathered Tyrolean caps, and greatcoats. Accessories, an integral part of every Göring outfit, reinforced this image, and artifacts such as the ancient Norse spear at right gave him the aura of huntsman extraordinaire.

As the Reich marshal's girth expanded, so did his wardrobe. By the mid-1930s, the closets of his four palatial homes were bursting with garments of every description, including silk underwear. Vain and frequently uncomfortable because of his weight, Göring changed finery as often as three or four times a day. Some of his many looks appear on the following pages.

A Uniform for Every Occasion

Göring's passion for designing, collecting, and wearing uniforms was legendary. For state and other ceremonial occasions, such as his lavish wedding to the actress Emmy Sonnemann *(right)*, full military dress was de rigueur. And every uniform was meticulously matched to the official business he was conducting, whether as the Reich marshal, the commander in chief of the Luftwaffe, or a leader of the National Socialist party.

This unending parade of spit and polish bemused and fascinated the German people, who joked that Göring was never completely naked. Even when he bathed, they jested, he wore rubber replicas of all his beloved medals and decorations in the tub.

Selections from a Bulging Wardrobe

Aware that Göring, unlike most senior Nazis, was a polished bon vivant, Hitler chose him to host visiting dignitaries. Göring threw himself into the role with sartorial gusto. For diplomatic functions, he appeared in white tie and tails, morning coat, or tuxedo; for greeting heads of state, he wore elaborate ensembles that included bejeweled daggers and other costly trimming; and for less formal occasions, he selected a tailored business suit or woolen knickers.

While frolicking with the elite at Karinhall, Göring pulled out all the stops. He greeted his guests in starched tennis whites, serenaded them in country attire, and showed off his art treasures wearing velvet knickers and gold-buckled shoes. Stuffed into a pair of lederhosen, he led visitors on a tour of his game preserve and ended the day wining and dining them while draped in a silken dressing gown.

Attempts on a Charmed Life

The year was 1939, and the event on the Nazi calendar was one that Adolf Hitler usually looked forward to—the annual reunion of participants in the Beer Hall Putsch. For several years, the Führer had returned to the now-famous Bürgerbräukeller in Munich on November 8 to deliver a self-congratulatory address to an enthusiastic crowd of original party members, the so-called *Alte Kämpfer*, or Old Fighters. On the following day, he led them through the city streets in a reenactment of the original march, striding behind the movement's most precious relic, the Blood Standard—the swastika flag allegedly stained with the blood of Nazi martyrs who had lost their lives in a hail of police bullets back in 1923.

But this November was different. The Reich was at war with Britain and France and was in the process of devouring conquered Poland. Hitler wanted the ceremonies scaled down. His deputy, Rudolf Hess, was scheduled to give the anniversary oration for him, and for security reasons the reenactment parade was canceled altogether. The previous year, only luck had prevented a young Swiss theology student named Maurice Bavaud from assassinating Hitler during the march. Just as Bavaud was about to draw his pistol, uniformed party members lining the curb in front of him raised their arms to hail the passing Führer and blocked the would-be assassin's view. (Bavaud walked away undetected but was later arrested on a train for traveling without a ticket. After his gun was discovered, the Gestapo interrogated him and extracted a confession. He was sentenced to death and beheaded.)

A day or two before the 1939 celebration, the Führer had a change of heart; he would deliver the speech after all. On November 8, he flew to Munich. Because of what he termed "important affairs of state," however, he wanted to return to Berlin that same night. To avoid the possibility that foggy weather might delay his flight, he decided to travel by a special train, which was scheduled to depart at 9:31 p.m. The new arrangements forced a change in the program. Instead of beginning his speech at 8:30 and speaking for an hour and a half, as he had done in previous years, Hitler would start thirty minutes early and limit himself to one hour.

Tumultuous applause interrupts Hitler during his speech at the Bürgerbräukeller in Munich on November 8, 1939—the sixteenth anniversary of the Beer Hall Putsch. Minutes after the Führer had finished speaking and left the building, a time bomb hidden in the pillar draped with the swastika flag exploded.

The decision saved his life—for concealed inside the column behind his podium was a powerful time bomb. It was the handiwork of one Georg Elser, a Swabian cabinetmaker with communist sympathies who had been plotting for months to kill Hitler. Even though the beer hall was now a Nazi shrine, patrons could come and go as they pleased during regular business hours. In April, Elser visited the hall and measured the column. He had already stolen some explosives and purchased ammunition from a rod-and-gun shop. In August, he became a regular customer, frequently hiding in the beer hall at closing time and emerging after everyone had left. Working stealthily in the deserted building, he sawed out a section of the wood paneling that covered the column. Each night, he removed the section and chipped away at the bricks and mortar. The next day, he carried out the debris in a small suitcase. After thirty-odd nights of secretive labor, Elser had fashioned a niche large enough for his bomb. On November 5, three days before the event, he installed the explosives and rigged them to detonate at precisely 9:20 p.m., when he expected Hitler to be in the middle of his oration.

Hitler's new timetable, however, foiled Elser's carefully laid plans. Thirteen minutes before the bomb went off, the Führer concluded his remarks and walked out of the beer hall. He was well on his way to the railway station when a massive explosion rocked the building, bringing down the ceiling over the rostrum where he had been standing. The blast killed a waitress and eight of the Old Fighters and injured sixty more. That night, Georg Elser was arrested by border guards as he tried to escape into Switzerland. He was sent to Dachau and survived until April 1945, when Hitler, in one of his final acts, ordered him killed.

Hitler was no stranger to narrow escapes. By his own count, Elser's bomb was the seventh attempt on his life. "I was suddenly overwhelmed by the feeling that I must return to Berlin that very evening," the Führer would later claim. "In fact, nothing important was waiting for me, but I heard this inner voice, which was my rescue. That I left the Bürgerbräu earlier than usual is proof that Fate wants to let me reach my goal!"

Despite such bravura statements that destiny was on his side, Hitler lived with a gnawing fear that some "criminal or idiot" might murder him before he was able to fulfill his mission. And after two narrow escapes in as many years, he wanted to take no unnecessary risks. He ordered the security precautions for his public appearances drastically tightened. Reinhard Heydrich, chief of the SS Central Security Office, developed the new procedures, which included constant surveillance of the sites that Hitler intended to visit, spot checks of traffic flowing into and out of the area, and preventive arrests of suspect persons. The strictures would make it virtually

At funeral services for party members who died in the beer-hall bombing, Hitler offers his sympathies to the widows of the victims. Nine persons were killed and sixty wounded in the blast.

impossible for a lone wolf, such as Bavaud or Elser, to get within killing range. Henceforth, if the Führer were to be eliminated, his killer would have to come from within his innermost circle. And there was only one group in Hitler's Reich that possessed the wherewithal to accomplish the job—the officer corps of the German army.

The army's leaders were slow to oppose the man who had returned them to prominence and who promised to restore Germany to greatness. Many of them applauded as Hitler ruthlessly went about reorganizing the nation—even though two of their number, Major Generals Kurt von Schleicher and Ferdinand von Bredow, had fallen victim to the Blood Purge of 1934, when Hitler destroyed the brown-shirted Storm Troopers as a quasimilitary force. The generals clung to their stiff-necked policy of *Über-*

parteilichkeit—nonpartisanship—and looked the other way. After the killings, they accepted Hitler's assurance that "in the state, there is only one bearer of arms, and that is the army." Moreover, as inheritors of the centuries-old tradition of obedience to the head of state, they felt bound by the solemn oath that all officers and men, from 1934 onward, had been obliged to take. "I swear by God this holy oath," they vowed, "that I will render unconditional obedience to the Führer of the German Reich and people, Adolf Hitler, supreme commander of the armed forces, and that I am ready, as a brave soldier, to risk my life at any time for this oath."

Serious opposition emerged only in late 1937, after Hitler revealed his plans for war to a small circle of top advisers at a secret conference in the Chancellery. When the minister of war, Field Marshal Werner von Blomberg, and the army commander in chief, General Werner von Fritsch, expressed the view that Germany was not ready for a war with the western powers, Hitler grew furious. He considered their opinions confirmation of what he had suspected all along—that the generals could neither grasp the new spirit of the times nor appreciate his genius. A German general, he believed, should be like a "butcher's dog that has to be held fast by the collar so it won't attack everyone in sight."

By early 1938, Hitler had driven both men from office: Blomberg for marrying a former prostitute less than half his age and Fritsch on a trumped-up charge of homosexuality. Seizing the opportunity to clean house, Hitler then pushed sixteen other generals into retirement and installed the ambitious but weak General Walther von Brauchitsch in place of Fritsch. He abolished the War Ministry and replaced it with a new office, the High Command of the Armed Forces (OKW), which was directly re-

General Ludwig Beck resigned as chief of the army high command and joined the Resistance because he feared that Hitler's proposed invasion of Czechoslovakia would drag Germany into an unwinnable war. "The anticipated success," he argued, "must justify the risk."

sponsible to him. For the chief of staff of the OKW, he selected the malleable General Wilhelm Keitel, who had served under Blomberg.

The diminution of the authority of the old army high command and the humiliation of Fritsch outraged the officer corps, especially Lieut. General Ludwig Beck, the chief of the army high command. Although Beck retained his position under Brauchitsch, he fought to clear Fritsch's name. A handful of senior generals, including Beck's deputy, Franz Halder, were plotting more drastic action: They wanted to confront Hitler, force him to withdraw his war plans, and stop the excesses of the SS and Gestapo. Halder asked Beck to join them, but the cautious fifty-seven-year-old Rhinelander declined. *"Mutiny* and *revolution,"* he explained, "do not exist in a German officer's dictionary."

Carl Friedrich Goerdeler *(right)*, the mayor of Leipzig, sits with Hitler in 1934. Three years later, Goerdeler resigned in protest after Nazis removed the statue of composer Felix Mendelssohn, a Jew, from its place opposite the Leipzig concert hall.

Within a few months, however, Beck was ready to take back his words. On May 28, 1938, Hitler approved a plan to invade Czechoslovakia. As a nationalist, Beck supported the goal of returning the Sudeten Germans to the fatherland through negotiation, but he feared that Hitler's actions would touch off a general war. In a memorandum to Brauchitsch, Beck wrote: "An attack on Czechoslovakia would bring Britain and France into the conflict at once. The outcome would be not only a military defeat, but a general catastrophe for Germany." In order to force Hitler to alter his course, Beck urged Brauchitsch to organize a mass resignation of senior generals. He spelled out the consequences if Germany's top officers failed to seize the moment. "Decisions vital to the future of the nation are at stake," he wrote. "History will indict these commanders for blood guilt if, in the light of their professional and political knowledge, they do not obey their conscience. A soldier's duty to obey ends when his knowledge, his conscience, and his sense of responsibility forbid him to carry out an order." Then he secretly contacted the governments of Great Britain and France to warn them of Hitler's plans.

When Brauchitsch refused to support him, Beck resigned. On August 27, he handed over his duties to Halder. Referring to his former deputy's treasonous plans during the Fritsch crisis, Beck admitted to Halder, "I realize now that you were right."

Beck determined to devote the rest of his life to thwarting Hitler. From his home in Berlin, he carefully set about organizing a resistance movement that involved an ever-widening circle of military officers and civilians. In addition to Halder, the group soon included General Erich Hoepner, the commander of the 1st Light Division; Admiral Wilhelm Canaris, the director of the Abwehr, the armed forces' counterintelligence agency; Lieut. Colonel Hans Oster, Canaris's chief of staff; and Lieut. General Erwin von Witzleben, the commander of the military district of Berlin. The senior police officials Wolf Heinrich Graf von Helldorf, the president of the Berlin police; Fritz-Dietlof Graf von der Schulenburg, Helldorf's vice-president; and Arthur Nebe, the director of the Reich Criminal Police Office, were also included, as were a number of influential civilians, such as Carl Friedrich Goerdeler, a former mayor of the city of Leipzig; Hjalmar Schacht, the former president of the Reichsbank; Hans von Dohnányi, a lawyer assigned to the Abwehr; and the diplomat Hans Gisevius, a former Gestapo officer now in the Ministry of the Interior.

Although the members of this diverse group could not agree whether to kill Hitler or merely arrest him, they set about plotting a coup d'état. A few days before the army marched on Czechoslovakia, Halder was to pass along the secret invasion date to the conspirators. Then General Witzleben's

Neville Chamberlain *(center)* **discusses the future of Czechoslovakia with Hitler in Munich in 1938. By acceding to Hitler's demands, the British prime minister foiled a possible coup d'état by the German army. "In shrinking from a small risk, Mr. Chamberlain made war inevitable," said a bitter conspirator.**

Berlin military-district troops and Helldorf's Berlin police would secure key positions in the city, seize Hitler, and declare a provisional government. The putschists in Berlin would be protected by General Hoepner's armored division, which was assigned to prevent the Leibstandarte SS Adolf Hitler, an SS division already on its way to the Czech border, from returning to Berlin and freeing the Führer.

The plan might have worked, but on September 29, 1938, the British prime minister, Neville Chamberlain, cut the ground out from under the plotters by capitulating to Hitler's demands at the Munich Conference. Czechoslovakia fell without a shot. Beck's group was not ready again to act against Hitler until after the conquest of Poland a year later. A major stumbling block remained: Without Brauchitsch's authority, Halder and the other schemers knew that the army rank and file would not support them. Halder, therefore delayed the coup until Brauchitsch had had an opportunity to convince Hitler of the military folly of an offensive against France. He banked on Brauchitsch joining them if the Führer refused his advice. But Hitler did more than that. Raging about the "spirit of Zossen" (the village south of Berlin where the army's headquarters were located), he tore apart Brauchitsch's arguments and cowed the army commander in chief into a full retreat. Fearful now that the Führer had gotten wind of the plot, Halder destroyed the plans for the coup.

In April and May of 1940, the Wehrmacht's stunning blitzkrieg victories in northern and western Europe raised Hitler's prestige to new heights. Because the masses, the Luftwaffe, and the army's junior officers stood solidly behind Hitler, Halder felt that a coup attempt could lead to civil war. Although he still despised Hitler, Halder withdrew his active support for Beck's group. "A breach of my oath to the Führer is not justified," he said. If any further attempts to overthrow the regime were made, he concluded, they would have to wait until Hitler had suffered a major military or political defeat that would diminish his popularity.

As Beck's loose assemblage began to fall apart, a few hard-core members turned their thoughts to assassination. The vice-president of the Berlin police, Schulenburg, made plans to kill Hitler during a victory parade in Paris in July, but the parade was called off because of the threat of a British air raid. The incident illustrated the increasing difficulties that were faced by the conspirators. As the war progressed, Hitler became less and less accessible. He refused to announce his schedule, was rarely seen in public, moved about under heavy guard, and canceled commitments at the last minute. Moreover, even if the Führer were eliminated, his Nazi henchmen would remain in power.

In vain, the conspirators continued to dispatch secret envoys abroad to seek encouragement from the Allies, who remained committed to total victory and were highly suspicious of opposition elements in the German military. Although they openly supported the resistance movements that sprang up in conquered lands, the Allied governments ignored the anti-Nazi movement inside Germany itself.

By late 1942, a growing awareness of the atrocities being committed daily in Poland and Russia combined with a downturn in Germany's military fortunes to attract important new members to the Resistance. They included Field Marshal Günther von Kluge, commander of Army Group Center on the eastern front, and General Friedrich Olbricht, deputy com-

Congratulating his generals after Germany's victory over Poland in 1939, Hitler extends his hand to Franz Halder, chief of the army high command (*far right*). Even then, Halder was conspiring to overthrow the Führer.

mander of the Reserve Army—home guards whose main responsibility was to train replacements for front-line troops.

December of 1942 brought the catastrophe that the Resistance had been waiting for. A Russian counterattack at Stalingrad cut off the German Sixth Army. As a direct result of Hitler's refusal to allow a retreat, 240,000 soldiers died or were captured. The scope of the defeat stunned the nation and infuriated the officer corps. Kluge's Army Group Center headquarters at Smolensk was already a hotbed of anti-Hitler sentiment. The leader of the malcontents was Colonel Henning von Tresckow, Kluge's chief operations officer. Tresckow assembled a handful of like-minded officers who vowed to act when Hitler came to visit in March.

A few days before Hitler's arrival, Admiral Canaris brought an Abwehr contingent to Smolensk, ostensibly to confer on intelligence matters. Its real purpose was to secretly coordinate the assassination of Hitler with a coup in Berlin—and to deliver to Tresckow a supply of pocketbook-size plastic explosives. The devices had been manufactured by the British for use by Allied partisans in Nazi-controlled Europe. Called clams because of their rounded, oblong appearance, the bombs worked better than similar German ones because their time-delay fuzes did not emit a warning hiss. Only one of the clams was powerful enough to twist a railway rail or crack the engine block of a truck.

Near the end of Hitler's visit, Colonel Tresckow asked a seemingly casual favor of Lieut. Colonel Heinz Brandt, an officer traveling on the Führer's airplane: Would Brandt be kind enough to carry two bottles of hard-to-get liqueur to his friend, Major General Helmuth Stieff, back at army headquarters in East Prussia? At the airfield that afternoon, Tresckow's aide, Lieutenant Fabian von Schlabrendorff, handed over the package. Instead of spirits, however, it contained four clams with a thirty-minute acid fuze. Just before giving up the package, Schlabrendorff broke the acid capsule by pressing a key against it.

Tresckow sent a coded message to Berlin that preparations for the coup should go forward. Several hours of agonized wait followed. Then came word that the Führer's plane had landed safely at Rastenburg, near his East Prussian headquarters.

Naturally, the conspirators feared that if the undetonated bombs were discovered, the plot would be exposed and all of them would face execution. Tresckow decided to telephone Brandt and simply tell him there had been a mix-up: He had sent the wrong package. The next day, Schlabrendorff took a regular courier plane, met the unwitting Brandt, and exchanged packages with him, handing over the liqueur bottles and walking away with the bombs. Boarding a train kept on a siding as accommodations for visiting staff, Schlabrendorff went to his compartment, locked

The sketches at right illustrate the security methods used to safeguard Hitler when he traveled by motorcade. While under way (top diagram), the Führer's limousine (red) was led by a pilot car (tan), 50 yards in front, and followed closely by two vehicles (green) loaded with SS Begleitkommandos, or escort guards. They, in turn, preceded an auto (orange) bearing SS officers. Any cars (blue) carrying additional VIPs followed 100 yards or more behind the convoy. Procedures for arriving, stopping, and departing are shown in the bottom diagram.

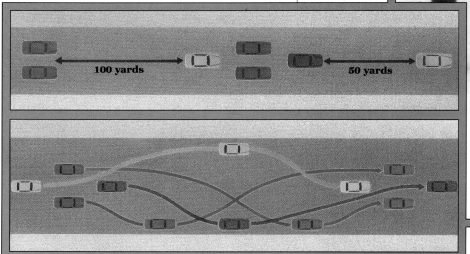

A triumphant but prudent Führer tours occupied Warsaw in an open Mercedes-Benz. Carloads of armed guards accompanied him, and hundreds of soldiers lined the route. Poles were forbidden to show their faces in the windows of the buildings.

The Führer's Airborne Command Post

Adolf Hitler called air travel a "necessary evil." Nowhere was he more vulnerable than when flying to and from his wartime headquarters. Yet he put great trust in his pilot, Hans Baur, and in his aircraft, a modified Focke Wulf FW 200 bomber dubbed the *Führermaschine*.

In 1937, the Reich Air Ministry had purchased one of the first FW 200 long-range transports for the Führer's exclusive use, but by 1942, a more secure aircraft was required, and a military version—the FW 200 Condor—was ordered. The new plane, shown here, was powered by four BMW-Bramo 323 R2 Fafnir engines and cruised at 160 miles per hour and had a range of 2,210 miles.

The *Führermaschine* seated eleven in addition to Hitler, whose compartment filled the center of the plane. Although the aircraft was armed with four MG 15 7.9-mm machine guns, an elaborate escape system *(inset)* was installed to enable Hitler to bail out through the floor if necessary.

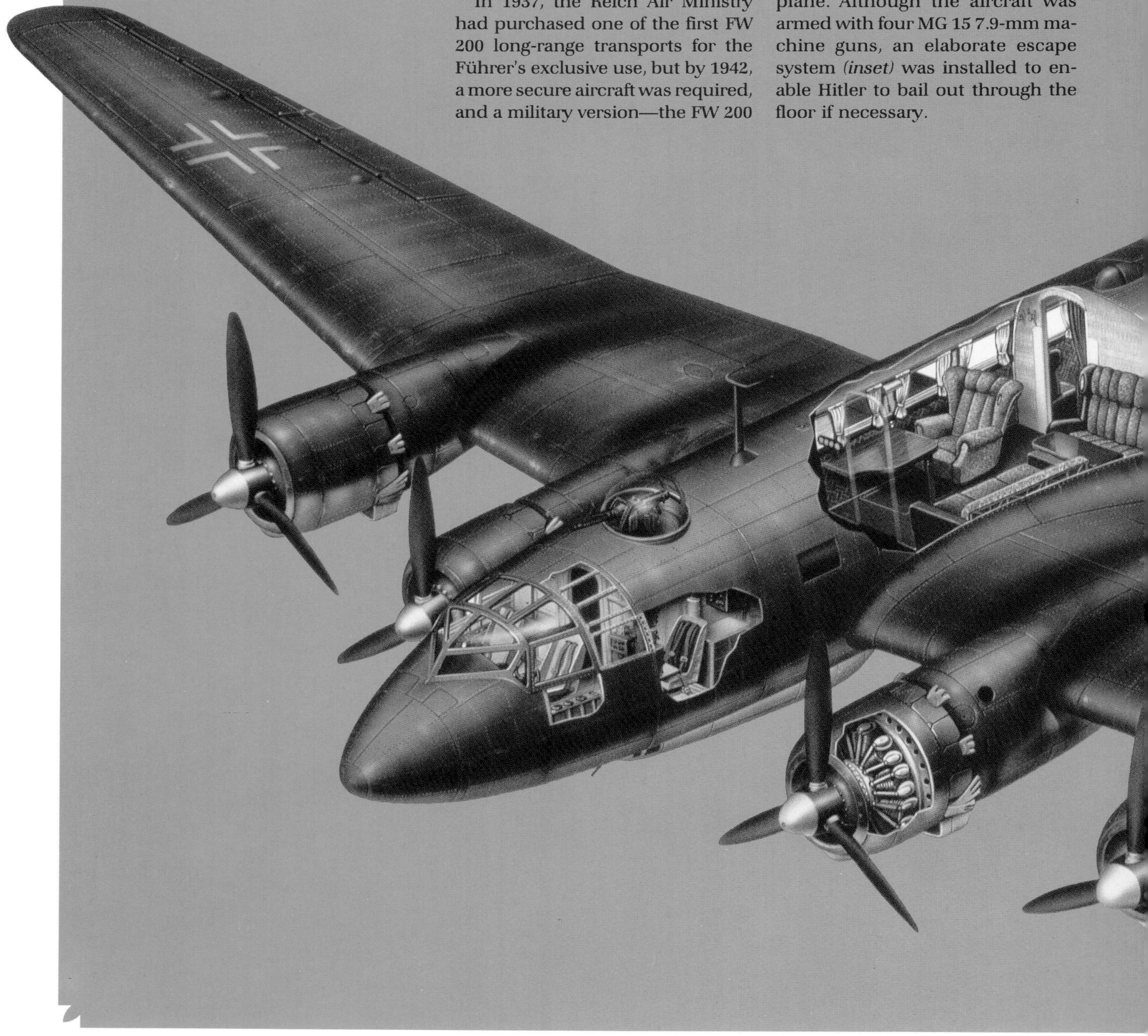

HITLER'S COMPARTMENT

1. Escape hatch
2. Chute lever for escape hatch
3. Oxygen tanks and hose
4. Worktable *(not shown)*
5. Fresh-air lever
6. Work lamp
7. Hitler's armchair
8. Parachute harness and lock
9. Reading lamp
10. Seat belt
11. Detachable rescue unit
12. Parachute container
13. Seat parachute

the door, and gingerly cut open the package with a razor. The fuze had worked, the firing pin had released, and the detonator had discharged. The plastic explosive was blackened but had not ignited. Evidently, cold air in the plane had prevented an explosion.

The conspirators tried again a week later. Hitler had designated March 21 *Heldengedenktag*, or Heroes' Memorial Day, to honor the dead of both world wars. He was scheduled to speak in the great hall of the Unter den Linden Armory in Berlin, then tour an exhibition of captured Russian weapons. Tresckow had arranged for a colleague from Army Group Center, Major General Rudolf von Gersdorff, to guide the Führer through the show. Gersdorff would be carrying a bomb with a ten-minute fuze. But once again, Hitler strayed from his schedule. After delivering his speech, he walked rapidly through the hall, barely looking at the hardware. Gersdorff had no opportunity to draw close. He saved his own life by stepping into a men's room and defusing the bomb.

By this time, many of the conspirators had come under suspicion. In April of 1943, the Gestapo arrested Schulenburg in Berlin and then released him. A few days later, Dohnányi was taken into custody; Oster was placed under house arrest; Beck and Gisevius were questioned but not held. Tresckow's work with the Resistance was interrupted when he was assigned to temporary command of a line regiment where he would have no contact with the Führer.

Throughout the eventful summer of 1943—as the Red Army counterattacked in the east and Mussolini fell from power in Italy, only to be propped up again by the German army—no further attempts were made on Hitler's life. Autumn, however, brought new opportunities and a new leader.

He was thirty-five-year-old Lieut. Colonel Claus Graf von Stauffenberg, scion of an aristocratic family, an intellectual, and a distinguished member of the high command. Like most officers, Stauffenberg initially had been impressed with national socialism, but by the time he had experienced the carnage in Russia and talked at length with Tresckow, he was convinced that Hitler was leading the nation to ruin. Before he could join the Resistance, however, he was transferred to North Africa, where in April 1943 he was severely wounded by machine-gun fire from a low-flying Allied plane. He lost his left eye, right hand, and two fingers of his left hand and damaged a kneecap. During his long convalescence, he decided to join the conspirators. When he returned to active duty in the fall, he was made chief of staff to General Olbricht. Part of his new job was to review and rewrite the orders that would mobilize the Reserve Army in the event of an emergency in Berlin. This Operation Valkyrie, as it was called, provided a perfect cover for organizing a coup d'état.

Stauffenberg threw himself into planning the coup. In addition to preparing the mechanics of killing Hitler, he had to recruit someone willing to do it. Stauffenberg found a candidate in Captain Axel von dem Bussche, a fellow veteran of the eastern front. During a tour of duty in the Ukraine, Bussche had been an inadvertent witness to a brutal atrocity. He had watched in horror as SS troops shot 5,000 Jews at the Dubno airfield. While the naked men, women, and children were herded to the slaughter, Bussche tried in vain to think of a way to stop the killing. He even considered ripping off his own clothes and joining the victims. The memory of the massacre haunted him, and he was prepared to sacrifice his life to exact retribution.

Maneuvering a captain of front-line troops into Hitler's presence, however, would not be easy. The opportunity came when a demonstration of some new uniforms and equipment was scheduled. A frequently decorated Nordic-looking combat veteran, Bussche was just the type to appeal to the Führer and thus was perfect for conducting the show. He would conceal a bomb inside his clothing. At the appropriate moment, he would pull the fuze and leap on Hitler, blowing up both of them.

Through November and December and into January of 1944, Bussche

Colonel Henning von Tresckow, operations officer for Army Group Center on the eastern front, tried to assassinate Hitler using a small, British-made bomb like the one at right. The availability of time fuzes complicated his planning; the only triggering devices at hand were acid ones that could be set for only ten or thirty minutes.

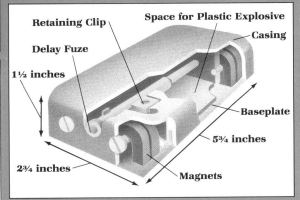

Retaining Clip

Delay Fuze

1½ inches

2¾ inches

Space for Plastic Explosive

Casing

Baseplate

5¾ inches

Magnets

Field Marshal Erwin Rommel watches with amusement as his superior, Field Marshal Gerd von Rundstedt, stoops to pet one of Rommel's dogs in the spring of 1944. Both men were aware of the army conspiracy against Hitler. Although Rundstedt refused to join, he encouraged Rommel to do so: "You are young and popular with the people," he urged. "You must do it."

held himself ready, but Hitler would not agree to a date; then an Allied bombing attack destroyed the equipment and uniforms intended for the demonstration. Bussche returned to combat and was wounded. During the subsequent weeks in the hospital, Bussche hid the bomb among his personal effects until he got a chance to pitch it into a lake.

Although Bussche was no longer available, the possibility of a uniform demonstration remained, and Stauffenberg was determined to take advantage of it. Another young officer—Lieutenant Ewald Heinrich von Kleist—was asked to consider sacrificing his life for the cause. The lieutenant sought advice from his father—a Prussian conservative and longtime opponent of the Nazis. The older man gave his blessing, and, thus prepared, Kleist waited for the demonstration to be scheduled.

By now, the Gestapo was closing in on the conspirators. In February of 1944, Canaris was removed from the Abwehr and placed under house arrest. Heinrich Himmler boasted to the admiral that he knew a plot was afoot and that he would crush it.

While Lieutenant Kleist chafed in the wings, Stauffenberg recruited another potential assassin, Captain Eberhard von Breitenbuch. On the afternoon of March 11, 1944, Breitenbuch was about to walk into a room behind Hitler and shoot him when a guard intervened. Though on the staff of Army Group Center, Breitenbuch had not been cleared for that particular briefing. Hitler was spared again.

In May, the plotters in Berlin and at Army Group Center received support from a new quarter, the western front. The military governor of France, General Karl-Heinrich von Stülpnagel, joined the conspiracy. Stülpnagel had tried hard to persuade his friend, Field Marshal Erwin Rommel, to use his influence to negotiate an end to the war in the west before the Anglo-American armies invaded Europe. The Resistance hoped that the widely admired Desert Fox would agree to become chief of state after Hitler was killed, but Rommel opposed the assassination. He argued that a dead Hitler would become a martyr and that a "stab-in-the-back" theory might arise—similar to the one many Germans associated with the defeat of 1918. Instead, Rommel believed Hitler should be arrested and tried publicly so the nation would learn of his crimes.

Meanwhile, Stauffenberg was still trying to recruit assassins. He was willing to make the attempt himself but had no access to Hitler. In June, however, that situation changed. Stauffenberg was appointed chief of staff to General Friedrich Fromm, who was Olbricht's superior and commander in chief of the Reserve Army. Stauffenberg's new duties would call for him to have frequent contact with the Führer. Now, for the first time, he made preparations to carry out the deed himself. He secured two packets of plastic explosives. Each one weighed about two pounds and had an acid fuze. The bombs fit neatly into his briefcase. Theoretically, it would be possible for him to start the fuzes, set the briefcase down near Hitler, and escape before the explosion.

Stauffenberg soon had an opportunity to assess his possibilities. On June 7, Hitler convened a conference at the Berghof. Stauffenberg attended and was encouraged to note that "in the Führer's immediate entourage, one has considerable freedom of movement." But time was running short.

Dismayed by the hopeless two-front war that Germany was fighting, Tresckow informed Stauffenberg: "The point now is not whether the coup has any practical purpose, but to prove to the world and before history that the German resistance is ready to stake its all. Compared with this, everything else is a side issue." Stauffenberg readily agreed. "Now it is not the Führer or the country or my wife and four children who are at stake," he declared; "it is the entire German people." The shame of doing nothing would be greater than failure.

The sense of urgency was heightened early in the month of July, when Julius Leber was arrested. Leber, a former Social Democratic politician and his party's defense expert, was slated to become minister of the interior after the coup. He knew most of the major participants, and if he broke under torture, all would be lost.

On July 7, the long-awaited equipment demonstration finally took place. Kleist could not get assigned to the event, however, and General Stieff, the only accomplice who was actually present, refused to be the assassin. The disappointments bore heavily on Stauffenberg. His nervous state alarmed a physician friend, who urged him to abandon the conspiracy. After all, he was not fully recovered from his war wounds yet, and in his weakened condition he might make serious errors of judgment. Stauffenberg refused to be deflected, nonetheless.

On July 11, Stauffenberg attended another briefing at the Berghof. This time, he carried the explosives in his briefcase. Everything had been prepared. An aircraft was standing by to help him get away. General Erich Fellgiebel, the chief of armed forces communications and a longstanding member of the conspiracy, was ready to notify the plotters in Berlin and sever communications with Hitler's headquarters. The plan called for killing Göring and Himmler as well, but neither showed up at the briefing, even though Himmler's SS was supposed to train the new reserve divisions being discussed. So Stauffenberg simply made his presentation and left—another opportunity wasted.

Three days later, Hitler returned to Wolfsschanze, his East Prussian field headquarters. The strain of almost five years of wartime leadership was wearing on him. He slept late, breakfasted alone, and at noon each day convened a briefing to review the military situation with his staff.

On the morning of July 15, Stauffenberg flew to the Rastenburg airfield servicing Wolfsschanze to participate in a series of briefings. The conspirators in Berlin placed the Operation Valkyrie forces on alert. Everything now depended on Stauffenberg, who confronted a situation of unimaginable difficulty. To arm the explosives, he would first have to open the briefcase and then, using pliers, break the capsule of acid that would activate the detonator ten minutes later—no small achievement for someone with only three fingers. After determining that he would be able to deposit the briefcase in the presence of both Hitler and Himmler, Stauffenberg would then have to create an opportunity to arm the bomb, rejoin the assembly, put down the briefcase, and escape.

During a break between briefings, Stauffenberg telephoned Olbricht's office in the capital city to say that he wanted to go ahead, even though Himmler would not be present. Olbricht delayed making a decision, then said he would call back. Colonel Albrecht Mertz von Quirnheim, Olbricht's chief of staff, was in the headquarters in Berlin. He thought the discussions that followed were "deliberately prolonged" and told his wife later that he had the "depressing feeling of finding myself alone"—with the exception of Stauffenberg, of course—"when the courage and determination to take the plunge were required."

After waiting as long as he could for an answer, Stauffenberg decided to

Major General Helmuth Stieff *(center)* **stands a few feet from Hitler during a demonstration of new field uniforms on July 7, 1944. Stieff's fellow conspirators hoped that he would take advantage of his proximity to kill the Führer with a bomb, but for reasons that still remain unclear, Stieff did not.**

go ahead on his own. By that time, however, the last briefing at which he could make the attempt was ending, and the opportunity was gone. Back in Berlin, Olbricht announced that the troop alert had been only an exercise and, as further cover, made an inspection tour of the units involved. For his part, Stauffenberg resolved that he would detonate the bomb the next time, no matter what.

By now, the western front was on the verge of collapse. Kluge and Stülpnagel considered withdrawing all German troops from the west and rushing them to the east to keep the Russians at bay while they concluded an armistice with Britain and the United States. Rommel agreed but insisted on confronting the Führer and giving him an opportunity to support the plan. Rommel drafted a letter to Hitler asking for the start of armistice negotiations, but before he could send it, his staff car was caught in the open by British fighter planes and he was seriously injured.

On July 20, 1944, Stauffenberg was ordered once again to Wolfsschanze. At dawn, along with his aide, Lieutenant Werner von Haeften, Stauffenberg boarded a Ju 52 at Rangsdorf airfield, near Berlin, for the 300-mile flight to Rastenburg. His briefcase was stuffed with papers for the briefing; Haeften carried the explosives.

A car met the two men and drove them the four miles to the compound—along a wooded lane secured at three places by checkpoints. It was a hot summer morning. After breakfast under an oak tree near the headquarters mess hut, Stauffenberg began a round of meetings: first, a general discussion of what was to be presented, then a conference with Keitel and, at 12:30, the Führer briefing.

By the time the meeting with Keitel began, about 11:30, young Haeften's nerves had frayed to the breaking point. He paced up and down the hallway outside Keitel's office, leaving the package of explosives unattended. An observant orderly on Keitel's staff noticed the package and asked what it was doing there. He accepted Haeften's explanation that it contained materials for the conference with Hitler.

By the time the officers emerged from Keitel's office for the quarter-mile walk to the briefing hut, it was almost 12:30. Stauffenberg asked if he could freshen up and change his shirt. He was directed toward a washroom. With Haeften in tow, Stauffenberg instead entered a nearby lounge, and the two men went to work. Haeften took out one packet of explosive, and Stauffenberg used pliers especially adapted to his awkward grip to break the acid capsule. They had ten minutes. Now for the second packet.

Keitel and his officers were waiting impatiently outside the building. At last, Keitel's adjutant, Major Ernst John von Freyend, ordered a sergeant to get Stauffenberg moving. The sergeant thrust open the door to the lounge

and gazed uncomprehendingly at the two men, who were bent over their briefcases in intense concentration. Hurry up! he urged. As the sergeant stood in the open door, Stauffenberg stuffed the armed bomb into his briefcase and left the second packet with Haeften. Then he hastened to join the others. John von Freyend reached for Stauffenberg's briefcase, apparently in order to help him, but Stauffenberg jerked it away with a determination that some of the onlookers remembered later. Haeften, meanwhile, went to find their getaway car.

Because the weather was hot, all five of the steel-shuttered windows of the briefing hut were open. The meeting was already under way. Lieut. General Adolf Heusinger, standing next to Hitler, was explaining the situation on the eastern front. Hitler, seated on a stool and absorbed in the maps that were spread before him on the heavy, wooden conference table, acknowledged Stauffenberg's arrival and turned back to the briefing. Stauffenberg quietly asked John von Freyend to help him get as close as possible to the Führer so that he could hear better. Obligingly, the adjutant led Stauffenberg to a position next to Heusinger. Stauffenberg coolly placed his briefcase underneath the table. Approximately five minutes had passed since the fuze had started.

Stauffenberg listened for a minute or so, then murmured something about having to make a telephone call. John von Freyend obliged him by taking him outside, where Stauffenberg said that he needed to talk with General Fellgiebel right away. The adjutant ordered an operator to place the call, then returned to the briefing. Stauffenberg picked up the receiver and, when the operator turned away, set it back down and left the hut. He walked 800 feet to a bunker, where Haeften and Fellgiebel were anxiously waiting with a car and driver.

They stood there for perhaps another minute. It was about 12:45. A tremendous explosion jolted them.

Stauffenberg and Haeften ducked into the car and ordered the startled driver to rush them to the airfield. They passed within a stone's throw of the demolished briefing hut. Stauffenberg said later that it looked as though a six-inch artillery shell had scored a direct hit. Hitler could not possibly have survived the blast.

At the first checkpoint on the airport road, Stauffenberg barked something about "Führer's orders" and was waved through. By the time the car reached the second checkpoint, the guards had received instructions not to let anyone pass. When the sergeant in charge refused to raise the barrier, Stauffenberg demanded to use the guardhouse telephone. He placed a call to a staff officer with whom he had shared breakfast that morning, and he spoke convincingly of the urgency of his mission to Berlin. The bluff worked. He handed the phone to the sergeant, who soon granted permission for the automobile to proceed. As they sped through the woods, Haeften tossed the second, unused packet of explosives out of the open car. At the third checkpoint, the men simply got out and walked the final distance to the airplane. By 1:15, barely half an hour after the blast, they were airborne for the capital city.

Fellgiebel, meanwhile, headed for the communications bunker to notify the conspirators in the capital that Hitler had been killed. Then he planned to sever communications between the headquarters and the outside world. Fellgiebel had not gone far when he saw a man stagger out of the smoke and dust, hair and clothes singed, face blackened, trouser legs hanging in tatters. It was Adolf Hitler. The Führer's right elbow was badly bruised, his eardrums punctured, but he was alive.

Hitler's remarkable luck had saved him once again. Had Stauffenberg used both packets of explosives, no one standing near the briefcase could have escaped with his life. But either because he was rattled by the sergeant who had walked into the lounge as he was arming the fuzes, or because he mistakenly believed the second packet would not detonate unless its own fuze was armed, Stauffenberg had reduced the force of the explosion by half. Then, the only place he could put the briefcase down without drawing attention to himself was against one of the table's massive supports—on a side away from Hitler. The blast had devastated the briefing room, mortally wounded four people, and burned and bruised the other twenty who were present. Nevertheless, its killing force had been dissipated through the open windows and deflected from the Führer by the thick tabletop and its sturdy support.

Fellgiebel was tormented by indecision. Hoping to urge the conspirators to go forward with the coup while not incriminating Stauffenberg in case everything fell apart, he telephoned a cryptic message to General Fritz Thiele, who was waiting at the conspirators' headquarters in the old War Ministry, now the armed forces high command, on Bendlerstrasse in Berlin: "Something fearful has happened. The Führer is alive." Then Fellgiebel ordered communications to and from Wolfsschanze restricted—an order that agreed with Hitler's wishes.

Fellgiebel's ambiguous message confused Olbricht. The plan was to announce the formation of a new government as soon as Hitler was dead. It would be headed by Beck, Goerdeler would serve as chancellor, and Witzleben would take over the armed forces. Martial law was to be declared, key government agencies and national broadcasting facilities seized, and the SS and Gestapo forces subdued. Fellgiebel had said the Führer was alive, though not in what condition. Was the "fearful thing" the assassination attempt, discovery of the plot, or something else? Unable to decide on a course of action, Olbricht and Thiele went out to lunch.

That afternoon, Benito Mussolini arrived by train at Wolfsschanze for a scheduled visit. Hitler not only kept the appointment but led his Italian ally on a tour of the demolished briefing hut. As he had five years earlier following the beer-hall explosion, Hitler took satisfaction from his brush with death. "After my miraculous escape today," he told Mussolini, "I am more than ever convinced that it is my fate to bring our great common enterprise to a successful conclusion." Mussolini concurred. It was, the duce said, a divine omen.

By the time Olbricht and Thiele returned from lunch, Berlin was seething with rumors. The communications blackout had broken down. At about 3:15, Stauffenberg and Haeften landed at a Berlin airfield. They called the conspiracy's headquarters to announce that Hitler was dead and to ask what progress had been made with the coup. No doubt dismayed by the answer, they drove to the headquarters, arriving about an hour later.

Olbricht continued to temporize. Perhaps he had expected Stauffenberg to shoot himself when the assassination failed, but Stauffenberg was back, and as Olbricht said later, in despair, "We cannot deny it now, can we?" Colonel Mertz von Quirnheim, Olbricht's chief of staff, pushed relentlessly for action. At his insistence, Olbricht at last took from his safe the written orders putting the coup in motion and began to issue them.

To be effective, the orders needed the signature of Fromm. Energized at last, Olbricht went to Fromm's office, told him that Hitler was dead, and asked him to sign orders for the Reserve Army to take measures against internal disturbances. Fromm had sensed the truth about the abortive July 15 alert and had been outraged by the foul-up, and he demanded proof that Hitler was dead. Olbricht arranged a priority call to Wolfsschanze. The telephone was answered by Keitel.

The rumors were nonsense, Keitel snapped. Hitler was fine. Fromm lapsed into frozen inaction.

Nevertheless, spurred by Mertz von Quirnheim, the Bendlerstrasse headquarters lurched belatedly ahead with the coup. At 4:30, about the time that Stauffenberg arrived, startled clerks began tapping out teletype orders to all military districts announcing the death of Adolf Hitler and the declaration of martial law under the supreme command of Field Marshal Witzleben. Because the orders were classified top secret, they had to be encoded and transmitted to each of the twenty districts one at a time. The process took three hours.

While the clerks worked, Stauffenberg issued a second set of orders, over Fromm's name but without Fromm's authority. They specified the meas-

Wearing a fresh uniform, Hitler appears shaken but not seriously injured several hours after the briefing-hut bombing. The chief of operations of the OKW, Colonel General Alfred Jodl *(with bandaged head)*, and Hitler's Luftwaffe aide, Colonel Nicolaus von Below *(at Jodl's left)*, also survived the blast. Had Stauffenberg been able to place the briefcase containing the bomb inside, rather than outside, the right table support, Hitler might have been killed. *(See diagram.)* Colonel Heinz Brandt, who died in the explosion, may have inadvertently saved the Führer by pushing the briefcase farther beneath the table *(gray line)*.

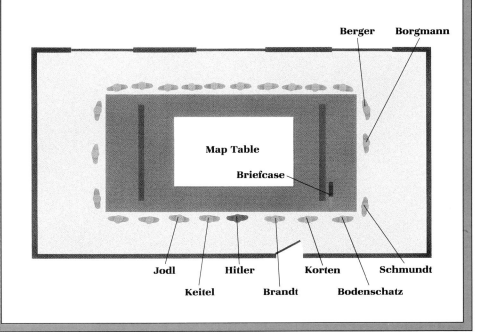

Berger Borgmann

Map Table

Briefcase

Jodl Hitler Korten Schmundt

Keitel Brandt Bodenschatz

ures to be taken by all commands to secure communications facilities, maintain law and order, and eliminate the SS and its branches. As these orders were being sent, Stauffenberg and Olbricht went with their aides to see the recalcitrant Fromm.

The confrontation turned out to be fiery. When Stauffenberg declared that Hitler was dead, Fromm shouted, "That is impossible! Keitel has assured me to the contrary!"

"Field Marshal Keitel is lying as usual," Stauffenberg retorted. "I myself saw Hitler being carried out dead." What is more, added Olbricht, orders for the Reserve Army to initiate Operation Valkyrie had already gone out. When Mertz von Quirnheim was called in to confirm the latter point, Fromm erupted in rage. He accused his officers of insubordination, revolution, and treason and declared them under arrest. Stauffenberg, said Fromm, should shoot himself at once.

Stauffenberg icily told Fromm to consider himself under arrest. Fromm responded by trying to physically attack his subordinates. He gave up only when faced with drawn pistols. Stauffenberg ordered Fromm placed in a side office under guard and resumed summoning the other coup leaders and the troops needed to secure Berlin. Before long, Beck and Hoepner arrived to assume their duties as head of state and commander of the Reserve Army, respectively.

Naturally, the orders to the military districts produced consternation across the Reich. Even though Witzleben had been a field marshal since 1940, he seemed an unlikely candidate for supreme command. District commanders who tried to confirm the orders with Fromm were told he was not available. And at about 6:00, the national radio began to announce repeatedly that an attempt on Hitler's life had been made and had failed.

Nevertheless, the conspirators made some progress. Reserve Army troops and police under their command occupied much of the central government district in Berlin and prepared to arrest Propaganda Minister Goebbels, the highest-ranking Nazi in the capital. German military commanders on the western front reacted vigorously; General Karl-Heinrich von Stülpnagel ordered 1,200 SS and Gestapo leaders in Paris rounded up and held for courts-martial.

The radio reports of Hitler's survival, the slow movement of the conspirators' military forces, and the arrival of countermanding orders from Wolfsschanze, however, all began to have their effect. Some subordinate officers doubted the legality of their orders. Major Otto-Ernst Remer, commander of the Greater Germany Guard Battalion, had been told that his troops were to help put down a grab for power by Nazi party officials. He went to see Goebbels—the man he had been ordered to arrest.

Not only did the quick-thinking Goebbels insist that Hitler was still alive, he called him up and put Remer on the telephone. When he heard the Führer's voice, Remer realized that his orders had been a hoax. Hitler ordered him to use whatever force was necessary to suppress the Resistance. Remer clicked his heels and complied. He ordered his men to disband the roadblocks that had sealed off the government buildings on Wilhelmstrasse, and he began to organize a defense against the coup. Troops sent to occupy radio transmitters in and around Berlin for the conspirators now secured them for the Führer.

Stauffenberg, Mertz von Quirnheim, and Olbricht labored feverishly into the evening. They reassured officers calling for confirmation of their orders; tried to determine the whereabouts of troops that were supposed to be in position; insisted to all that Hitler was dead, despite radio announcements to the contrary; and attempted to gain the cooperation of the many staff officers, not previously involved, whose services were essential to the revolt. While they worked, Beck waited to take over administration of the country. Field Marshal Witzleben, supposedly the army's new supreme commander, was nowhere to be found.

When Hans Gisevius, who had been promised a senior post in the new Germany, arrived at the Bendlerstrasse headquarters, he was shocked by the confusion. Milling around would not do, he declared. "We must have some corpses now!" Instead of waiting for troops to command, he said, the officers should shoot Goebbels and Gestapo chief Heinrich Müller. But it was too late: The conspirators were rapidly losing control of what forces they had mobilized, and loyal troops were moving on Bendlerstrasse.

When Witzleben finally turned up, at about 8:00, he was at first refused entrance to the building by sentries who did not recognize him. Once inside, his first words to Stauffenberg were "This is a fine mess." After complaining loudly about the efforts being carried out in his behalf, Witzleben left in a huff and went home.

Around 9:00, staff officers who were not conspirators demanded to see Olbricht. They wanted an explanation of the discrepancies between their orders and the news on the radio. Instead of explaining, Olbricht urged them to defend the building. Dissatisfied, the staff officers, led by Lieut. Colonel Franz Herber, asked to see Fromm.

The general had done little to hinder the coup. Now, however, braced by the loyal officers, Fromm was prepared to try to resume control. He strode back into his office to find Beck, Olbricht, Hoepner, Stauffenberg, Mertz von Quirnheim, and Haeften being held at gunpoint by the loyalists. "Well, gentlemen," said Fromm to the conspirators, "I am now going to do to you what you did to me this afternoon." He demanded their weapons

Speaking to the nation from Wolfsschanze at one o'clock in the morning on July 21, Admiral Karl Dönitz pledges the navy's loyalty

to the Führer. Hitler, seated between Bormann and Jodl, opened the broadcast by explaining how the bomb plot had failed.

and said they were about to be tried by a court-martial consisting of the other officers present and himself. Beck requested permission to retain his pistol "for personal use." Fromm told him to be quick about it. Beck raised the pistol to his temple and fired. Gravely wounded but conscious, Beck fired again, then fell to the floor unconscious but still alive. A sergeant delivered the coup de grâce.

Fromm asked whether the others had any last wishes. Olbricht and Hoepner—the latter denying that he had anything to do with the coup— asked permission to write statements. They dragged out the task for half an hour before Fromm lost patience, announced that they were all condemned to death, and ordered them downstairs into a courtyard. Stauffenberg made a brief statement assuming all responsibility; the others, he said, had acted under his direct orders. Then they all went to their fate except Hoepner, who talked Fromm into sending him to jail instead.

In the courtyard, drivers of several vehicles were ordered to park their cars so that the headlights illuminated a mound of dirt next to a nearby building project. Olbricht was placed in front of the mound and shot by a ten-man firing squad. Stauffenberg was led into position, faced his executioners, and shouted, "Long live holy Germany!" As the rifles cracked, Haeften lunged forward into the bullets. The squad reloaded and shot Stauffenberg. Mertz von Quirnheim was the last to die.

Fromm made a speech to the soldiers in the courtyard, who were now part of a cordon of loyalists around the Bendlerstrasse headquarters. He thrice called out, "Sieg heil!" then drove away to report his achievements to Goebbels. His reward from the SS was immediate arrest and eventual execution by a firing squad.

Shortly after midnight, about the time Stauffenberg and his colleagues were being shot, the voice of Adolf Hitler crackled across the airwaves. He had survived a "crime unparalleled in German history," he rasped. After naming Stauffenberg as the would-be assassin and stating that the conspiracy had nothing to do with the spirit of the German people, Hitler declared, "We shall get even with them in the way to which we National Socialists are accustomed."

Now the SS was turned loose. Late in the evening, Himmler had arrived from East Prussia and established headquarters in Goebbels's home. One of his first moves was to have the bodies of the five men shot by Fromm exhumed, burned, and their ashes scattered. Under the command of Colonel Otto Skorzeny, the swashbuckling commando leader who a year earlier had rescued Mussolini from captivity, a special detachment of troops began making wholesale arrests.

Not only the participants in the coup, but many innocents were appre-

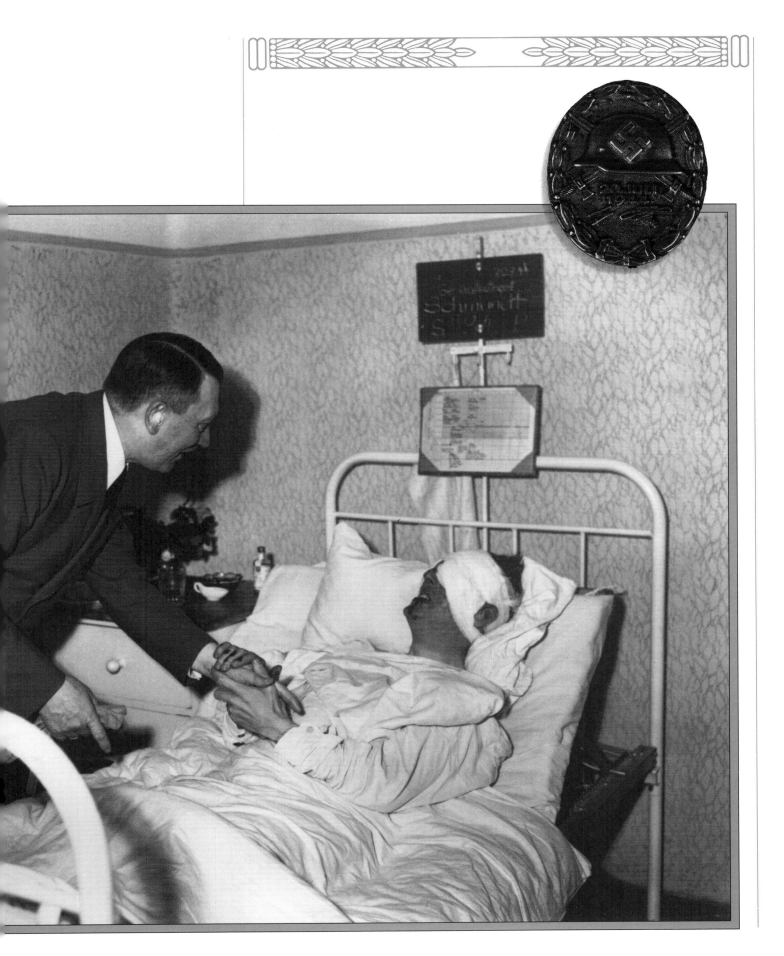

hended. Himmler invoked an alleged tradition among ancient Aryans— "We shall introduce here absolute responsibility of kin," he said. "Let no one say, 'What you are doing is bolshevistic.' It is not bolshevistic at all, but an old custom practiced by our forefathers. You can read about it in the Teutonic sagas." Himmler vowed that the Stauffenberg family would be exterminated. Scores of relatives, from toddlers to the elderly, not only of Stauffenberg but of dozens of others involved in the plot, were hunted down and herded into concentration camps. Some of the leading conspirators were arrested almost immediately—among them Witzleben, Fellgiebel, Oster, Canaris, and Schacht.

When Tresckow and Schlabrendorff at Army Group Center's headquarters learned of the failure, Tresckow resolved to kill himself. He set out alone toward the front lines and blew himself up with a grenade. His last words might have been an epitaph for all those in the Resistance: "We have done the right thing. In a few hours, I shall stand before my God, responsible for my actions and my omissions. I believe I shall be able to say with a clear conscience that I have done my best in the struggle against Hitler. God will, I hope, spare Germany because of what we have done."

Schlabrendorff, who did not believe in suicide, was arrested and brutally tortured. A metal device with spikes was attached to his hands and legs; each time he refused to answer a question, the device was screwed tighter and the spikes penetrated deeper. Then, with his arms bound to his side, Schlabrendorff was forced to kneel and clubbed repeatedly from behind until he struck the floor facefirst. He resisted as long as he could, then gave information only about Tresckow, who he knew was already dead.

Despite the barbaric methods used to make prisoners talk, the Gestapo was slow to piece together a comprehensive list of participants. Bussche, Gersdorff, and Breitenbuch, three officers who had volunteered for suicide missions to assassinate Hitler, were never arrested. Diplomat Hans Gisevius went into hiding and eventually escaped to Switzerland.

For a time, the conspirators in France maintained an understanding with the local SS, based on the fact that all concerned had thought the July 20 orders from Bendlerstrasse were legitimate. Then Kluge, trying to save himself, implicated Stülpnagel. Summoned to Berlin, Stülpnagel had his driver stop along the way, walked out by the old Verdun battlefield, and shot himself. Unfortunately, the general succeeded only in blinding himself. He was arrested and executed a month later, but not before, while delirious from his wound, he uttered the name Rommel over and over. By October, the famous field marshal's association with the conspirators had been confirmed. The news stunned the Führer, because Rommel had always been one of his favorites. On October 17, SS troops surrounded

Former Field Marshal Erwin von Witzleben, who was to become commander of the Wehrmacht after the coup, struggles to hold up his beltless prisoner's trousers during his trial before the People's Court on August 8, 1944. He was condemned and executed that same day.

Rommel's home village near Ulm, and two officers presented him with a choice: A show trial in the capital, followed by death for him and persecution for his family, or a dignified suicide, a state funeral, and enduring honor. Rommel chose suicide, and the Nazi government fulfilled its part of the bargain *(pages 169-171)*.

Although Kluge had overseen the arrest of a dozen or more plotters, he could not escape suspicion himself. Relieved of command in France on August 17 and summoned to Berlin, he, too, stopped at a point along the old western front and swallowed a cyanide capsule.

For those who did not choose suicide, the government staged show trials in the People's Court in Berlin. They were presided over by Judge Roland Freisler, a sadist whom Hitler proudly called "our Vishinsky," a reference to Stalin's chief prosecutor during the notorious Moscow purge trials of the 1930s. The first officers, Field Marshal Witzleben among them, went on trial August 7. "They must be tried at lightning speed," fumed Hitler, "and not be given a chance to make any grand speeches. They are not to receive the honorable bullet," he went on. "I want them to be hanged like common traitors and strung up like butchered cattle."

Freisler swiftly condemned the defendants. The next day, they were taken to a room in Plötzensee Prison, where a row of meat hooks had been secured to a beam across the ceiling. From the hooks dangled hangman's nooses fashioned from thin, strong cord. Each condemned man was lifted off the floor and strangled by his own weight. A camera crew recorded the executions and sent the film by courier to Hitler at Wolfsschanze. In all, about 200 men, most of them army officers, were tried and executed. Across the country, scores of others were hanged, beheaded, or shot to death with even less pretense of a trial.

Fabian von Schlabrendorff, the officer at Army Group Center who had been so cruelly tortured, was one of the few conspirators to survive. After several delays, his trial was scheduled for February 3, 1945, the same day Allied bombers raiding the capital city scored a direct hit on the People's Court. Judge Freisler numbered among those killed. Schlabrendorff was unharmed. He was eventually sent to the concentration camp at Flossenbürg to be shot, but the approach of American troops prompted the camp commandant to evacuate his prisoners. Schlabrendorff was transferred to Dachau and ultimately to South Tyrol, where the Allies took him into custody as the war came to an end.

Hitler's merciless retribution weakened the army in the hour of its greatest trial. Inexperienced loyalists replaced veteran officers who lacked sufficient party credentials to suit the Nazis. All staff officers were required to spend precious time politically indoctrinating their subordinates. The Hitler salute, which had been voluntary, was made mandatory "as a sign of the army's unshakable allegiance to the Führer and of the close unity between army and party." Thus merged, the army, the party, and Germany descended toward destruction, led by a man who clung to the belief that his escapes from death were, in the end, "confirmation of the task imposed upon me by Providence." ✚

Rommel's funeral procession passes through the ancient city gates of Ulm, bringing his body from the nearby family home.

Trumped-Up Tribute to a Fallen Hero

Rarely did Nazi cynicism run deeper than in the funeral accorded Field Marshal Erwin Rommel, a national hero and one of Hitler's favorites. Rommel was pressured into committing suicide after being linked, at least indirectly, to the July 20 plot against Hitler. In order to obscure the truth about his death, he was given a posthumous tribute worthy of a Wagnerian warrior.

Rommel's death had been orchestrated with similar care. In October 1944, Hitler sent two generals and an escort of SS men to Rommel's home near Ulm, where he was recuperating from head wounds suffered in Normandy. The officers gave him the choice of being tried before the People's Court and shot, or taking poison. If he chose suicide—and died still apparently faithful to Hitler—his family would be spared reprisals. To protect his wife, Lucie, and their son, Manfred, Rommel swallowed a poison capsule. His body was driven to a hospital, where officials announced he had died of his earlier wounds.

Having arranged Rommel's demise, Hitler ordered a full-blown military funeral, which was photographed by a young man in the crowd. His pictures are shown here and on the following pages. Officers from all the armed services and a guard of honor came to Ulm by special train. Field Marshal Gerd von Rundstedt, Rommel's superior on the western front, represented the Führer, who sent a huge wreath.

Perhaps most painful for members of the Rommel family, who knew the truth, were the messages from Hitler, Göring, and other ranking Nazis. "The most despicable part of the whole story," Manfred Rommel wrote, "were the expressions of sympathy we received" from the men who had caused the death of his father.

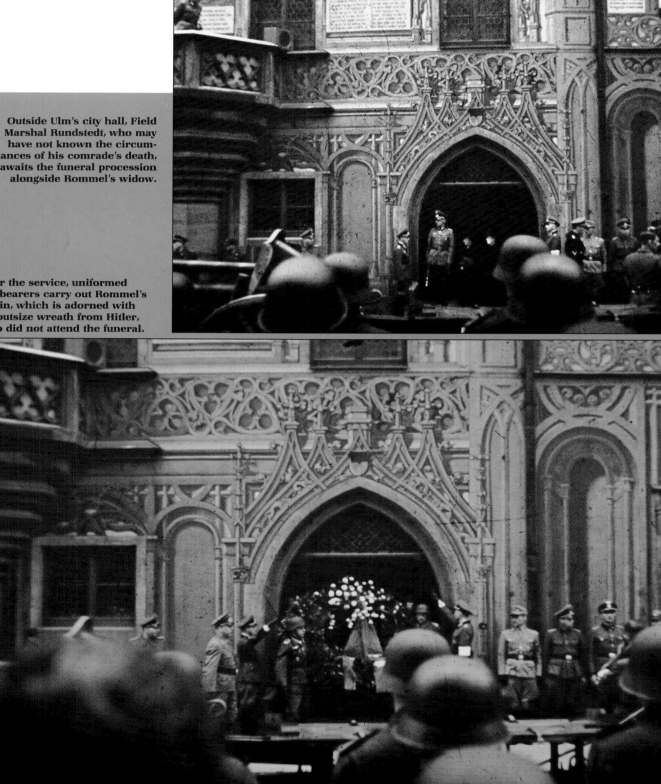

Outside Ulm's city hall, Field Marshal Rundstedt, who may have not known the circumstances of his comrade's death, awaits the funeral procession alongside Rommel's widow.

After the service, uniformed pallbearers carry out Rommel's coffin, which is adorned with an outsize wreath from Hitler, who did not attend the funeral.

Rommel's helmet and the field marshal's baton Hitler had conferred on him two years earlier rest poignantly atop the flag-draped casket, which is transported on a gun carriage in traditional military fashion.

Partners in Adversity

By chance, Adolf Hitler's honored guest at Wolfs-schanze on July 20, 1944—the day of the assassination attempt—was his beleaguered ally, Benito Mussolini. The relationship between the two dictators had been curiously warm and enduring. Mussolini had marched to power in Italy in 1922, a decade before Hitler's rise, and Hitler had saluted the duce in *Mein Kampf* as the father of fascism and "one of those lonely men of the ages on whom history is not tested, but who are themselves the makers of history."

Although they embraced a common ideology, the two leaders were an unlikely pair. The barrel-chested Mussolini cut an imposing figure in his gaudy, well-tailored uniforms. By contrast, Hitler was physically unprepossessing and dressed so plainly as to seem shabby by comparison. Gregarious and outgoing, the duce took delight in the ostentatious trappings of a latter-day Caesar. Hitler, on the other hand, affected a Spartan lifestyle. Socially reserved and ill at ease, his rambling monologues rarely conveyed the passion expressed in his public speeches.

In the early years of their association, Mussolini patronized the Führer as an inspired but intellectually awkward protégé. "Hitler clearly idolized Mussolini," the duce's wife recalled, "but my husband was more reserved about Hitler." Mussolini once disparaged Hitler as a "muddleheaded fellow" whose political philosophy was "utterly incoherent." The duce considered his alliance with the German Reich a marriage of convenience and resented the fact that Berlin, not Rome, had become the capital of world fascism.

By the summer of 1944, Mussolini's fortunes had plummeted. Ousted from power a year earlier, the duce had been arrested by the new Italian government, which signed an armistice with the Allies and declared war against Germany. SS commandos had rescued Mussolini from his mountain prison and installed him as puppet ruler of a state in northern Italy. At the age of sixty-one, Mussolini had dwindled to a shadow of his robust self when he arrived seeking small favors from his former junior partner in the Axis alliance, who on this day had reason to sense his own mortality.

Hitler and Mussolini exchange lighthearted banter on the

railroad platform at Rastenburg, East Prussia, three hours after Hitler was injured in an assassination attempt.

An aide displays the shrapnel-torn trousers of an officer wounded in the blast.

Wreckage from a Near Miss

Adolf Hitler greeted Benito Mussolini at Rastenburg with the words, "Duce, an infernal machine has just been let off at me." Although his injured right arm trembled slightly and his ears were stuffed with cotton, the German leader immediately insisted on taking his visitor on a tour of the bomb-shattered briefing room at Wolfsschanze.

Hitler seemed strangely elated, like a survivor of combat, as he displayed his singed scalp and shredded clothes. "Look at my uniform! Look at my burns!" he exclaimed. When Mussolini expressed amazement that anyone could have survived the blast, Hitler assured his ally that his deliverance was an omen of victory for "our great common enterprise." The Führer's confidence proved contagious. "This was a sign from heaven," Mussolini said. "What has happened here today gives me new courage."

The duce flinches at the sight of the

conference room. A witness said: "Mussolini was absolutely horrified. He could not understand how such a thing could happen."

Hitler confers with Heinrich Himmler as Mussolini and Göring follow.

Reich Marshal Göring and Foreign Minister

An Emotional Parting

In the course of the hour-long meeting between the German and Italian delegations, Hitler's mood fluctuated from moody silence to raging imprecations against those who had betrayed him. The session was further marred by an acrimonious dispute between Hermann Göring and Joachim von Ribbentrop, whom Göring derided as a "dirty little champagne salesman."

Nevertheless, Hitler was obviously comforted by Mussolini's presence and repeatedly stressed his lasting friendship and admiration for the fascist leader. The feeling was reciprocated. "When I have a friend," Mussolini stated, "I march together with him to the end."

At seven in the evening, Hitler escorted Mussolini's party to the train that would bear the former Italian strongman south to an uncertain future. In a rare display of personal warmth, Hitler raised his uninjured left arm and grasped the hand of his ally. "I know that I can count on you," Hitler said, "and I beg you to believe me when I say that I look on you as the best and possibly only friend I have in the world." The two would not meet again.

Ribbentrop look on as Hitler and Mussolini say good-bye at the Rastenburg station.

Acknowledgments and Picture Credits

The editors thank: Federal Republic of Germany: Berlin—Klaus Dettmer, Landesarchiv; Heidi Klein, Bildarchiv Preussischer Kulturbesitz; Gabrielle Kohler, Archiv für Kunst und Geschichte; Wolfgang Schäche; Wolfgang Streubel, Ullstein Bilderdienst. Bonn—Michael Oberstadt, Friedrich-Ebert-Stiftung. Grosshansdorf—Heinz Höhne. Hamburg—Jochen von Lang. Koblenz—Meinrad Nilges, Bundesarchiv. Munich—Elisabeth Heidt, Süddeutscher Verlag Bilderdienst; Robert Hoffmann, Presseillustrationen Heinrich R. Hoffmann. German Democratic Republic: Berlin—Hannes Quaschinsky, ADN-Zentralbild. United States: District of Columbia—Elizabeth Hill, Robert Wolfe, National Archives; Eveline Nave, Library of Congress; George Snowden, Snowden Associates. New Jersey—Al Collett. Virginia—Ray O. Embree, Jr. *Inside the Third Reich* by Albert Speer reprinted with permission of Macmillan Publishing Company and Weidenfeld & Nicolson, Ltd. Copyright © 1969 by Verlag Ullstein GmbH; copyright © 1970 by Macmillan Publishing Company (translation); copyright © 1970 by Weidenfeld & Nicolson, Ltd. (translation).

Credits from left to right are separated by semicolons, from top to bottom by dashes. Cover: Roger-Viollet, Paris. 4: Süddeutscher Verlag Bilderdienst, Munich. 6, 7: Hugo Jaeger, LIFE Magazine, © Time Inc. 10, 11: Presseillustrationen Heinrich R. Hoffmann, Munich. 13: Uliy Povolotskiy, courtesy Soviet Army Museum, Moscow—from *World War II German War Booty* by Thomas M. Johnson, published privately by author, 1984. 14, 15: Presseillustrationen Heinrich R. Hoffmann, Munich. 16: FPG International. 19: Bundesarchiv, Koblenz. 20, 21: Süddeutscher Verlag Bilderdienst, Munich—from *The New Germany, 1933-1945*, by Mike and Mark Chenault, Taylor Publishing Company, Dallas, 1971, Chenault and Speer. 22, 23: Presseillustrationen Heinrich R. Hoffmann, Munich. 25: Bildarchiv Preussischer Kulturbesitz, West Berlin—Globe Photos, N.Y. 26-31: Presseillustrationen Heinrich R. Hoffmann, Munich. 34, 35: Hugo Jaeger, LIFE Magazine, © Time Inc. 36, 37: Ullstein Bilderdienst, West Berlin; from *Die Neue Reichskanzlei: Architekt Albert Speer*, Franz Eher Nachf., GmbH, Munich, 1940 (2). 38-45: From *Die Neue Reichskanzlei: Architekt Albert Speer*, Franz Eher Nachf., GmbH, Munich, 1940. 46: FPG International. 49: Map by R. R. Donnelley and Sons Company, Cartographic Services. 50: Presseillustrationen Heinrich R. Hoffmann, Munich. 52, 53: AP/Wide World Photos. 54: Private collection. 55: Presseillustrationen Heinrich R. Hoffmann, Munich. 56: Bildarchiv Preussischer Kulturbesitz, West Berlin. 59:

Landesbildstelle, West Berlin. 60, 61: Dr. Wolfgang Schäche, West Berlin, except lower left from *The New Germany, 1933-1945*, by Mike and Mark Chenault, Taylor Publishing, Dallas, 1971, Chenault and Speer. 62, 63: Presseillustrationen Heinrich R. Hoffmann, Munich—*Der Stürmer*, courtesy Bildarchiv Preussischer Kulturbesitz, West Berlin. 64: Photographs by Steve Tuttle, courtesy of private collection (2)—photograph by Steve Tuttle, courtesy of Neil Hardin. 65: Ullstein Bilderdienst, West Berlin. 66: Ullstein Bilderdienst, West Berlin—FPG International. 69: Süddeutscher Verlag Bilderdienst, Munich. 71: Hugo Jaeger, LIFE Magazine, © Time Inc. 72, 73: Presseillustrationen Heinrich R. Hoffmann, Munich. 74: Barnaby's Picture Library, London. 76: AP/Wide World Photos. 78: From *Leaders and Personalities of the Third Reich* by Charles Hamilton, R. James Bender Publishing, San Jose, 1984. 79: Hugo Jaeger, LIFE Magazine, © Time Inc. 80: Toland Collection; Presseillustrationen Heinrich R. Hoffmann, Munich—from *Hitler* by Joachim C. Fest, Harcourt Brace Jovanovich, Inc., New York, 1974. 81: Ullstein Bilderdienst, West Berlin—Süddeutscher Verlag Bilderdienst, Munich. 82: Süddeutscher Verlag Bilderdienst, Munich. 83: Bildarchiv Preussischer Kulturbesitz, West Berlin—Popperfoto, London. 84: Süddeutscher Verlag Bilderdienst, Munich; Heinrich R. Hoffmann, LIFE Magazine, © Time Inc. 85: Courtesy Time Inc. Picture Collection; Martin Munkácsi. 86-87: AP/Wide World Photos—from *Eva Braun* by Johannes Frank, Verlag K. W. Schutz, Preussisch Oldendorf, 1988; Keystone, Paris—Süddeutscher Verlag Bilderdienst, Munich. 88, 89: National Archives, no. 242-EB-24-15B—no. 242-EB-1-43E; no. 242-EB-4-42B; no. 242-EB-5-44A. 90: Presseillustrationen Heinrich R. Hoffmann, Munich—National Archives, no. 242-EB-8-39C. 91: Archives Tallandier, Paris—National Archives, no. 242-EB-12-2; no. 242-EB-12-16B. 92, 93: Presseillustrationen Heinrich R. Hoffmann, Munich—National Archives, no. 242-EB-13-40A; National Archives, no. 242-EB-6-19C; AP/Wide World Photos. 94: Presseillustrationen Heinrich R. Hoffmann, Munich. 98, 99: Hugo Jaeger, LIFE Magazine, © Time Inc. 100: Bildarchiv Preussischer Kulturbesitz, West Berlin. 101: Presseillustrationen Heinrich R. Hoffmann, Munich. 102-103: Presseillustrationen Heinrich R. Hoffmann, Munich; Richard Schulze-Kossens, Düsseldorf. 104: Süddeutscher Verlag Bilderdienst, Munich. 105: FPG International—The Bettmann Archive. 106: Map by R. R. Donnelley and Sons Company, Cartographic Services. 110-116: Presseillustrationen Heinrich R. Hoffmann, Munich. 118: Presseillustrationen Heinrich R. Hoffmann,

Munich—from *The Bormann Letters*, edited by H. R. Trevor-Roper, Weidenfeld & Nicolson, London, 1954, courtesy of François Genoud. 119: Ullstein Bilderdienst, West Berlin. 120, 121: Bildarchiv Preussischer Kulturbesitz, West Berlin. 122-125: Ullstein Bilderdienst, West Berlin. 126, 127: Presseillustrationen Heinrich R. Hoffmann, Munich. 128: Bundesarchiv, Koblenz; Presseillustrationen Heinrich R. Hoffmann, Munich; Ullstein Bilderdienst, West Berlin—courtesy George A. Petersen, reproduced from the collections of the Library of Congress. 129: Courtesy George A. Petersen, reproduced from the collections of the Library of Congress; Bildarchiv Preussischer Kulturbesitz, West Berlin, foto Hoffmann—from *The Reich Marshal* by Leonard Mosley, Doubleday & Co., Inc., New York, 1974. 130: Ullstein Bilderdienst, West Berlin—Library of Congress; from *Signal* Magazine, January 1941, courtesy George A. Petersen—courtesy George A. Petersen, reproduced from the collections of the Library of Congress (2). 131: Ullstein Bilderdienst, West Berlin—Süddeutscher Verlag Bilderdienst, Munich; Bildarchiv Preussischer Kulturbesitz, West Berlin, foto Hoffmann. 132: Presseillustrationen Heinrich R. Hoffmann, Munich; Bundesarchiv, Koblenz; Süddeutscher Verlag Bilderdienst, Munich; Heinrich R. Hoffmann, LIFE Magazine, © Time Inc. 133: Süddeutscher Verlag Bilderdienst, Munich; courtesy George A. Petersen, reproduced from the collections of the Library of Congress; Edimedia, Paris. 134: Barnaby's Picture Library, London. 136, 137: The Hulton-Deutsch Collection, London. 138: Bildarchiv Preussischer Kulturbesitz, West Berlin. 139: From *Das Dritte Reich/Zweiter Weltkrieg*, no. 47. 140, 141: Bundesarchiv, Koblenz. 143: Presseillustrationen Heinrich R. Hoffmann, Munich. 144: Artwork by William J. Hennessy, Jr.; Presseillustrationen Heinrich R. Hoffmann, Munich. 146, 147: G. Klawek, Hagen; artwork by Stansbury, Ronsaville and Wood, Inc. 149: Ullstein Bilderdienst, West Berlin—artwork by William J. Hennessy, Jr. 150: From *Rommel* by Richard D. Law and Craig W. H. Luther, R. James Bender, San Jose, 1980. 153-155: Ullstein Bilderdienst, West Berlin. 159: Ullstein Bilderdienst, West Berlin—art by William J. Hennessy, Jr., courtesy Imperial War Museum, London. 162, 163: Presseillustrationen Heinrich R. Hoffmann, Munich. 164, 165: Presseillustrationen Heinrich R. Hoffmann, Munich; Stephen D. Wolf/N. Neil Hardin Collection, Long Beach, California. 166, 167: Ullstein Bilderdienst, West Berlin. 169-171: Volker Schmeissner. 172, 173: Ullstein Bilderdienst, West Berlin. 174, 175: Presseillustrationen Heinrich R. Hoffmann, Munich; Ullstein Bilderdienst, West Berlin. 176-177: Ullstein Bilderdienst, West Berlin.

Bibliography

Books

Backes, Klaus, *Hitler und die Bildenden Künste*. Cologne: DuMont Buchverlag, 1988.

Below, Nicolaus von, *Als Hitlers Adjutant, 1937-45*. Mainz, W.Ger.: v. Hase & Koehler Verlag, 1980.

Berg-Pan, Renata, *Leni Riefenstahl*. Boston: Twayne, 1980.

Briffault, Herma, ed., *The Memoirs of Doctor Felix Kersten*. Transl. by Ernst Morwitz. Garden City, N.Y.: Doubleday, 1947.

Bullock, Alan, *Hitler: A Study in Tyranny*. New York: Harper Torchbooks, 1964.

Cooper, Matthew, *The German Army, 1933-1945*. London: Macdonald and Jane's, 1978.

Cowdery, Ray, *Hitler's New German Reichschancellery in Berlin, 1938-1945*. Küsnacht, Switzerland: Northstar Maschek, 1987.

Davidson, Eugene, *The Trial of the Germans*. New York: Macmillan, 1966.

Dietrich, Otto, *Hitler*. Transl. by Clara Winston and Richard Winston. Chicago: Henry Regnery, 1955.

Fest, Joachim C.:
The Face of the Third Reich. Transl. by Michael Bullock. New York: Pantheon Books, 1970.
Hitler. Transl. by Clara Winston and Richard Winston. New York: Harcourt Brace Jovanovich, 1974.

Forty, George, *German Tanks of World War II 'in Action.'* London: Blandford Press, 1988.

François-Poncet, André, *The Fateful Years*. Transl. by Jacques LeClercq. New York: Harcourt, Brace, 1949.

Frischauer, Willi, *The Rise and Fall of Hermann Goering*. Boston: Houghton Mifflin, 1951.

Gilbert, Felix, *Hitler Directs His War*. New York: Octagon Books, 1982.

Grunfeld, Frederic V., *The Hitler File*. New York: Random House, 1974.

Gun, Nerin E., *Eva Braun*. London: Leslie Frewin, 1969.

Halder, Franz, *Hitler as War Lord*. Transl. by Paul Findlay. London: Putnam, 1950.

Hamilton, Charles, *Leaders and Personalities of the Third Reich*. San Jose, Calif.: R. James Bender, 1984.

Heiber, Helmut, *Goebbels*. Transl. by John K. Dickinson. New York: Hawthorn Books, 1972.

Heiden, Konrad, *Der Fuehrer*. Transl. by Ralph Manheim. Boston: Houghton Mifflin, 1944.

Hitler's Secret Conversations, 1941-1944. New York: Farrar, Straus and Young, 1953.

Hoffmann, Heinrich, *Hitler Was My Friend*. Transl. by R. H. Stevens. London: Burke, 1955.

Hoffmann, Peter:
German Resistance to Hitler. Cambridge, Mass.: Harvard University Press, 1988.
The History of the German Resistance, 1933-1945. Transl. by Richard Barry. London: Macdonald and Jane's, 1977.
Hitler's Personal Security. Cambridge, Mass.: MIT Press, 1979.

Hutton, J. Bernard, *Hess*. New York: Macmillan, 1971.

Irving, David, *Göring*. New York: William Morrow, 1989.

Johnson, Thomas M., *World War II German War Booty*. Columbia, S.C.: Johnson Reference Books, 1982.

Kramarz, Joachim, *Stauffenberg*. Transl. by R. H. Barry. New York: Macmillan, 1967.

Lang, Jochen von:
Adolf Hitler. New York: Harcourt, Brace & World, 1969.
The Secretary: Martin Bormann. Transl. by Christa Armstrong and Peter White. New York: Random House, 1979.

Langer, Walter C., *The Mind of Adolf Hitler*. New York: New American Library, 1973.

Leasor, James, *The Uninvited Envoy*. New York: McGraw-Hill, 1962.

Littlejohn, David, and C. M. Dodkins, *Orders, Decorations, Medals and Badges of the Third Reich*. Mountain View, Calif.: R. James Bender, 1968.

Manvell, Roger, *The Conspirators: 20th July 1944*. New York: Ballantine Books, 1971.

Manvell, Roger, and Heinrich Fraenkel:
Hess. New York: Drake, 1973.
Himmler. New York: G. P. Putnam's Sons, 1965.

Maser, Werner, *Hitler*. Transl. by Betty Ross and Peter Ross. London: Allen Lane, 1973.

Mosley, Leonard, *The Reich Marshal*. New York: Dell, 1975.

Peterson, Edward N., *The Limits of Hitler's Power*. Princeton, N.J.: Princeton University Press, 1969.

Picker, Henry, *The Hitler Phenomenon*. Transl. by Nicholas Fry. London: David & Charles, 1974.

Picker, Henry, and Heinrich Hoffmann, *Hitler Close-Up*. Transl. by Nicholas Fry. New York: Macmillan, 1973.

Pryce-Jones, David, *Unity Mitford*. New York: Dial Press, 1977.

Seabury, Paul, *The Wilhelmstrasse*. Berkeley: University of California Press, 1954.

Semmler, Rudolf, *Goebbels*. London: Westhouse, 1947.

Shirer, William L., *The Rise and Fall of the Third Reich*. New York: Fawcett Crest, 1962.

Smelser, Ronald, *Robert Ley*. Oxford: Berg, 1988.

Snyder, Louis L., *Encyclopedia of the Third Reich*. New York: Paragon House, 1989.

Speer, Albert, *Inside the Third Reich*. Transl. by Clara Winston and Richard Winston. New York: Collier Books, 1981.

Toland, John, *Adolf Hitler*. New York: Ballantine Books, 1981.

Waite, Robert G. L., *The Psychopathic God: Adolf Hitler*. New York: Basic Books, 1977.

Warlimont, Walter, *Inside Hitler's Headquarters, 1939-45*. Transl. by R. H. Barry. New York: Frederick A. Praeger, 1964.

Wheeler-Bennett, John W., *The Nemesis of Power*. London: Macmillan, 1964.

Wilmot, Chester, *The Struggle for Europe*. New York: Harper & Brothers, 1952.

Wistrich, Robert, *Who's Who in Nazi Germany*. New York: Bonanza Books, 1984.

Wykes, Alan, *Himmler*. New York: Ballantine Books, 1972.

Young, Desmond, *Rommel*. New York: Quill, 1978.

Zentralverlag der NSDAP, *Die Neue Reichskanzlei: Architekt Albert Speer*. Munich: Franz Eher Nachf., 1940.

Zoller, Albert, *Hitler Privat*. Düsseldorf, W.Ger.: Droste-Verlag, 1949.

Other Publications

"Aggrandizer's Anniversary." *Time*, May 1, 1939.

"Herr Hitler's Birthday." *The Times*, April 20, 1939.

"Hitler Parades Reich Might at Fete." *The New York Times*, April 21, 1939.

National Archives. "Eva Braun's Diary with English Translation."

Index